If Being

Raised In An Orphanage

Was So Bad ...
Why Did I Like It So Good

Gene Bishop

A thought provoking and inspiring book about
being raised at a children's home

"If Being Raised In An Orphanage Was So Bad, Why Did I Like It So Good" *By: Gene Bishop*

All proceeds from this book
will be donated to the
Sam Smith Endowment,
Connie Maxwell Children's Home,
Greenwood, South Carolina

FOREWORD

Gene Bishop is a goal-oriented leader. Almost three years back he declared his intent to write about his childhood at Connie Maxwell Children's Home. Any potential income from the effort would benefit this institution he loves and supports. This book is the accomplishment of his goal. Readers will want to recognize it for what it truly is—an effort to say thanks and to affirm the good , which came to one young life because others cared.

As the current president of Connie Maxwell, Gene afforded me the privilege of writing a foreword to his work. My joy at doing so flows from my affection for Gene and the "Orphanage" family from which he hails as well as my undying respect for the strong yet tender ministry that was home for him and his peers.

Putting thoughts in writing is always a bit risky, especially if these thoughts recount one's own journey through life. For the courageous, looking back through the telescope of years provides new and broader understanding of things and events. Blessed is the person who can look back with a smile on his face and gratitude in his heart.

Gene possesses the most invaluable data for evaluating the credibility of children's homes: personal experience. His testimony in these pages, in full harmony with those of many others like him, is that life in a children's home (orphanage) can be largely positive. The memories he shares are real, colorful, and cherished. He liked his time at the orphanage not because he was a martyr or oriented toward masochistic

3

pleasures. He liked it because it was safe, nurturing, relational, and fun.

Some adults choose to ignore or even deny their pasts. Others offer the stories of their youthful lives as examples of what happens when the grace of God, the benevolence of mankind, and the triumph of the human spirit collide. Gene Bishop's contribution is of this latter type.

As you read these pages, celebrate the fact that many displaced children are continuing to find hope and healing. Remember also that it is never too late to have a happy childhood.

Jimmy McAdams
President
Connie Maxwell Children's Home
Greenwood, South Carolina

DEDICATION

I have been fortunate to have many mothers and fathers in my life. Today we refer to these individuals as "mentors." I think I have had literally hundreds. They have caused me to be successful and are responsible for me being where I am today. This list could fill many pages. The list could start with the many staff members at Connie Maxwell that encouraged me and always had something complimentary to say to me or about me. It could include a list of teachers and professors that took an extra interest in me. It could include a list of some of my fellow Connie Maxwell alumni that were my brothers and sisters. It could include a list of my family members who in their own quiet way showed me their love.

I know I will make a lot of people happy when I say, "I hereby dedicate this book to Dr. Sam Smith"-- who was my "father," my mentor, my disciplinarian, my confidant. The one person that I could always turn to and who always listened to me.

"Dr. Sam" (as we called him) had a smile that could melt a glacier, a heart as big as the whole campus, a tenderness that was as soft as a butterfly with sore feet, a demeanor as genuine as a saint, and a voice that said, "I care." Kids would flock around him like little puppies following their mother – he would be followed anywhere he would go on campus. He was our leader, our light at the end of the tunnel, our hand to hold to in the dark. Dr. Sam went on to his reward in heaven on December 18, 1997. I dreaded that day and hoped it would never come. I often wondered how I would react when he died. I think I surprised myself. My wife, Pat, and I got to the church about an hour early on the Sunday afternoon of the funeral. I was able to just sit and think about all the people he had touched in his lifetime -- the most unique peace came over me -- I thought I would be a nervous wreck, but I wasn't. I sat on a pew for about an hour thinking about how a part of him would never die. Hundreds of children all over the United States are alive, healthy, and successful because of "Dr. Sam."

----Gene Bishop

"He who pursues righteousness and love finds life, prosperity and honor." Proverbs 21:21 NIV

My thanks to these special people- - -

- To my wife, Pat who was my constant "critic." She typed, re-worded, re-worked, made suggestions, offered solutions, stayed up late, and a hundred other things that made this book possible. I sometimes think she loves Connie Maxwell more than I do.
- To Mack Baltzegar, Scott James, Harold Driggers, John Sheriff, and Dean Mahaffey for always being there when I needed them.
- To Dr. Jimmy McAdams who sat and listened to me lay out my plan. He offered suggestions, made recommendations, and encouraged me all along the way.
- To Joan Bunch who typed and typed and retyped. She edited, offered suggestions, and made changes that helped this book "come alive."
- To all of my brothers and sisters who returned my questionnaire and told their story about what Connie Maxwell meant to them.
- Last, but certainly, not least - to all the staff at Connie Maxwell who have loved, cried, lost sleep, felt joy, been rejected, wondered "why" a thousand times, I say a special thank-you. Your job is often thankless but so totally indispensable. You are the real authors of this book. It is your book. Thank you for doing a thousand things that you never get credit for doing. You can know assuredly that God does not miss a single one of those acts of kindness.

                                              ---Gene Bishop

7

OPENING REMARKS

I would like to give you a quick view of things you will read in this book and things that you will not read.

You Will Read

1. A sometimes heart's wrenching account as told by several Connie Maxwell Alumni about how they came to be at Connie Maxwell.

2. Fabulous stories by former Connie Maxwell alumni who achieved heights of success with an attitude of "whatever comes my way, I'll handle it."

3. Some inspiring and motivating stories and ideas that not only changed the lives of some alumni but also the lives of the people around them.

4. About a journey of faith, hope, and resolve that will inspire you to look a little deeper into your own heart and soul.

You Will Not Read

1. A series of negative and inflammatory stories about bad things that happened at Connie Maxwell.

2. An account of why some things happened like they did – this book is not a psychoanalysis of the why's and wherefore's.

3. A take off on "what might have been, if only."

WHEN AND WHERE IT ALL BEGAN

Chapter 1

I've learned that the more a child feels valued, the stronger his values will be.

September 12, 1997, I celebrated an event that happened fifty years earlier. I don't believe I will ever forget the colors of purple and orange that filled the sky that day as my father drove away from the front of the Eastern Star Home at Connie Maxwell Children's Home in Greenwood, SC. It was September 12, 1947. I remember through my tears seeing the tail end of his 1946 Chevy and the dust (the roads at Connie Maxwell were not paved at that time) around the car as he disappeared down the road. I felt abandoned, hurt, and alone. I don't think I have ever felt so alone in my entire life. I was twelve years old going on twenty. My mother had died in March of that year and (even though I didn't know it at the time) she had asked my dad to send us three children to Connie Maxwell. I think she felt that he would not be able to raise us. I was born the second of three children – my brother, Harold, was seventeen months older and my sister, Maxene, was five years younger than I was. We all went to Connie Maxwell on September 12, 1947. My brother and I were placed at Eastern Star Home and my sister was sent to Martha Smith Home.

In 1947, grades one through seven were in the old school building on campus. Grades eight through twelve were sent to Greenwood County Schools. So my first two years at Connie Maxwell were spent almost entirely on campus since I was in the sixth and seventh grades. It was a very protected environment and I remember being off the campus only on very special occasions.

Those first two years at Connie Maxwell were a very sensitive time in my life. I was terribly homesick and not a very happy camper. I did not adjust very well at all. My brother ran way several times and eventually left Connie Maxwell to live with my father. Maxene, my sister, was only six years old when we came to Connie Maxwell. Those years together created a unique bond between us. Maxene stayed at Connie Maxwell until she finished high school. She went on to Lander College and received BS in education and later earned her Master's Degree at Furman University. She is currently retired and does volunteer work for the American Red Cross and others.

Mrs. Windham was the cottage mother at Eastern Star Cottage and she ruled it with an iron fist. All the boys were afraid of her and for good reason. She acted as though she was mad at somebody or something most of the time. She was a big woman with a very overpowering and intimidating stance, posture, and walk. She wore big broad-heeled shoes and you could hear her walking down the hall even when you were out in the yard. The walk reminded me of a soldier walking in high step fashion. All of us "little" boys considered the walk as positive because it always gave us some warning that she was coming our way. If we were doing something that was against the rules (or something she didn't want us to do), that walk gave us enough time to hide. Or even to stop, run, get under the bed, or make our get away – which ever was most appropriate at the time, depending on what we were "into."

I'm sure that you have gathered by my first few remarks that we weren't perfect little angels. Even though she was very strict on us, it was out of necessity - with twenty-one boys under your "command," you can't always be saying please for every little thing you want done.

We had three big bedrooms - one for the little boys, one for the medium sized boys, and one for the big boys. The big boys were responsible for keeping the little and medium sized boys in <u>line</u>. As I look back on that situation now, I think that was the only way you could keep order. If you let your mind wander just a little, you can imagine twenty-one boys ranging in ages from six to seventeen years under one roof with all the demands that each one may have. Twenty-one boys using the bathroom (or trying to use it). Twenty-one boys getting all their books together to take to school. Twenty-one boys eating breakfast (at three big huge round tables — seven to a table by size and age). Twenty-one boys -- all trying to talk at the same time. And, one cottage mother saying, "<u>enough is enough</u>." Looking back on that situation, I think I would have been a basket case if I had been in her shoes. Somehow we took it all in stride - "I think."

I don't think there has ever been a young boy or girl that came to Connie Maxwell that can say, "<u>all of my experiences were positive</u>." I don't think any boy or girl who was raised in a normal home, with normal parents, that had a normal income, with normal friends, that went to a normal school and was involved in normal community and church activities can say "all of my experiences growing up were positive." Almost no one grows up without some bad, negative or tragic experiences, wherever the individual "<u>grows up</u>." The simple act of "<u>growing up</u>," no matter where it takes place, is fraught with some good and some bad. I will cover some of those ideas in a later chapter entitled *"Is Being An Orphan A Plus or A Minus?"*

11

The sixth grade was very hard for me. School had already started by September 12, 1947 when I arrived on campus. I came into the classroom knowing no one. I was the "new" boy. I wasn't sure if I should be meek, mild, belligerent, authoritative, or quiet. I'm not sure my teacher or fellow classmates knew exactly what to do with me. I didn't want to appear scared, but I was. I didn't want to fight either. My classmates didn't know it at the time, but I had failed the second grade. My father took all of us in 1944 to Panama City, Florida where he worked in a shipyard. It was during the Second World War and every man and woman in the United States was very deeply involved in winning the war. Women worked in maintenance, airplane, tank, jeep, rifle, and textile factories. They did whatever was necessary to supply the fighting men with what they needed to win the war. We had to go to school in shifts when we arrived at Panama City. I went to school from 7:00 a.m. to noon. The second shift went from noon to 5:00 p.m. We moved around a lot that year and I lost so much school time, I failed the second grade. I was ridiculed and embarrassed because I was perceived as a "failure." I didn't know until years later what really happened and why. At that time in my life, I considered that incident a stumbling block – today I see it as a stepping stone.

Let's go back to the sixth grade classroom. I sensed on my first day in class that all of us had something in common – we had no family. One of the oddest and strangest things was we seemed reluctant to share with each other why we were there. I'm not completely sure, to this day, why that attitude prevailed. I'm not sure that our awareness level was all that high—but I think down deep we realized that we weren't all there for the same reason. Some were there because their parents (one or more) were in prison. Some were there because one of the parents was deceased (which was my case). Some were there because the family had become dysfunctional because of alcohol, drugs, or severe health problems. Some were there because they were effectively abandoned. Whatever the reason, we immediately felt like we had just stepped into a room full of friends. Effectively they were the "family" that we weren't suppose to have – so we became instant brothers and sisters.

We still fussed with each other. We had disagreements, we fought, we growled and, in general, we did most things that brothers and sisters do. This was our loose knit family, but not so loose knit that if a "outsider" picked on one of "us", they could get away free and clear. We would fight for each other like any brother and sister. I have often told people I come in contact with that I hold a world's record for having the most brothers and sisters. In the late forties and early fifties, there were approximately three hundred to three hundred fifty boys and girls on campus. We had enough children to have full blown football, basketball and baseball teams; and I might add, we were pretty tough to deal with. We were told constantly to "mind your manners" and "play fair"—but one "unwritten" rule was "we weren't going to take any guff off of anybody we played against, just because we were living at a children's home.

From 1892 to 1947 Connie Maxwell was know as "Connie Maxwell Orphanage." In 1946 the South Carolina Baptist Convention felt that a more appropriate name should be "<u>Connie Maxwell Children's Home</u>."

Connie Maxwell was named after the daughter of Mr. & Mrs. John Maxwell. She died when she was seven years old of scarlet fever and her parents were so distraught by her death, they donated approximately four hundred acres of land just outside of Greenwood, South Carolina to be known as <u>Connie Maxwell Orphanage</u>. If they could come back on campus today and see all the children that have been helped and all the programs that exist to help and heal hurting children, I'm sure they would stand and look in total disbelief. What a blessing that has developed from the death of a frail little seven-year old girl named Connie.

I stayed at Eastern Star Home for three years – from 1947 to the summer of 1950. In the summer of 1950, I got up enough nerve to go to "Dr. Sam" Smith, the superintendent of Connie Maxwell at that time, to ask him to move me to another cottage. I felt like I was taking my life in my own hands by doing this — I was bucking a very dominating woman, Mrs. Windham. I realized I could run faster than she could so I had to take the chance. My personality and hers were like trying to make oil and water mix together. It hadn't worked in three years and I didn't think it would work in another fifty years. I really wanted to work on the farm but I was so little (I only weighed one hundred six pounds the day I graduated from high school) they thought I couldn't handle the job.

Dr. Smith granted my request and moved me to the "chicken farm." It wasn't exactly what I wanted but I sure wasn't about to turn it down. The boys who worked on the chicken farm were responsible for gathering the eggs, killing and dressing the frying chickens, vaccinating the other chickens, and anything else that Mr. "Hawk" Hawkins needed done. The chicken farm was looked on as a "sissy" job but that sure didn't bother me. It put me back <u>to nature</u>, which I loved. After being on the chicken farm for about a year, I started rotating to the vegetable farm for one month and the cattle farm the next month. Mr. Bill Clyburn was in charge of the vegetable farm and Mr. Dick Rhodes was in charge of the cattle farm. Both Mr. Clyburn and Mr. Rhodes were very good to work for and Mr. Rhodes was special to me.

The cattle farm had about five hundred beef cattle in the early 1950s. Mr. Rhodes needed someone to check the cattle everyday, seven days a week, three hundred sixty-five days a year. I wanted to be that person. I didn't mind the work and didn't mind the time spent on our new horse, "<u>Nelle</u>." Mr. Rhodes gave me the job and I felt that I was in heaven. It took anywhere from 1-1/2 to 3 hours every day, including Saturday and Sunday, to check the cattle. I looked for any sign of new births, hurt and/or crippled cows, diseases, or cows that had been attacked or killed by a pack of wild dogs we had in the area. I felt like I had been appointed CEO to the biggest corporation in America. I wouldn't have swapped that job for all the money in the state.

I was willing to take on any amount of responsibility that Mr. Rhodes would give me. Whatever Mr. Rhodes asked me to do, I would do it. I think that is the reason we hit it off so well together.

I always wanted a little extra money in my pocket so I would work for thirty-five cents an hour on Saturday afternoon instead of going to town to see a movie or just getting off campus.

One incident that particularly stands out in my mind while I was working on the chicken farm involved Easter time and different colored dyed little chicks. The local farm and garden store had several hundred dyed chicks that they couldn't sell. So after Easter the manager called Dr. Smith and asked if he wanted them. Dr. Smith must have been thinking about me. He asked if I wanted to raise them until they became fryers (frying sized chickens). I told him I did and they were delivered to the chicken farm. They were red, blue, green, purple, orange, and about ten others colors that I don't even remember. The little barn where the chickens were placed had to be lighted and kept temperature controlled. The chicks had to be fed and watered several times a day. Our cottage was only seventy-five to one hundred feet from where the chicks were housed. The chicks were very young and would "imprint" on any human that was taking care of them. In effect I became their mother. I had to be very careful that I didn't step on one every time I walked into the chicken house. They always tried to follow me every where I went. In my absence, they would huddle together in order to keep warm. As they were huddling together, invariably one or two would get trapped, couldn't breath and would die. I kept a very close record of the number of chicks the farm supply store had given us; and how many of them died from huddling. If my memory serves me right, I lost ten to fifteen chicks in the raising process out of about three hundred. Mr. Hawkins told me that was an excellent record. You can imagine how big my ego grew. As time went on, the "colored chicks" matured and we found out they were "white leggans." Their feathers were all white, even on their legs, hence their name—"white leggans."

I have often wandered why this "chicken" incident was so important to me. After starting this book, I think I now realize that Dr. Smith wanted me to have the responsibility of completely taking care of something and experiencing the satisfaction of hard work and the joy it can bring. I don't think I will ever forget all those colored "little chicks" and how they followed me everywhere I went. I guess that was the first time I experienced "chicken love."

This little incident reminds me of how important animals are to children and now much therapy and growth can come from taking care of and being involved with animals.

Dr. Jimmy McAdams in 1998 developed just such a program involving animals and gardening called OASIS, which stands for OUTDOOR ADVENTURES SPECIFICALLY INVOLVING STUDENTS.

As a trustee of Connie Maxwell, I was first exposed to the program through one of our trustee meetings. I immediately thought about my personal experience with "Nelle", with checking the cows and with raising the colored chicks. Those programs were most helpful to me personally. I have said to Dr. McAdams on more than one occasion how creative his ideas were. I think it has tremendous application for positive therapy for children at Connie Maxwell today. I think it could be an outstanding positive effect at any institution like Connie Maxwell.

Another very positive incident that happened to me in the seventh grade was the "Declaration Contest." Dr. Herring, the principal at our campus elementary school, encouraged me to enter the annual "Declaration Contest." Those who entered had

17

to compete against each other by giving a speech and/or learning or memorizing some famous speech given by a famous person. I chose the "Gettysburg Address" by Abraham Lincoln. I didn't realize how short it was until I read it again recently. But in the seventh grade, I though it was eight miles long at least, if not more. I memorized and memorized and then rehearsed and rehearsed over and over and over. I thought I had it down pat until I stepped on the stage that morning. I froze and almost walked off the stage but my teacher, Mrs. Timmerman kept telling me how good I was going to do. She helped settle me down. I stumbled through it somehow and won the contest.

That experience surely impacted my life in a significant way. Today (August 2000) I speak to audiences all over the southeastern United States through my company, People & Solutions, Inc.

The events that happened to me at Connie Maxwell keep coming back to me time and time again. My whole life, to this day, continues to be shaped in a very positive way by these "little" events.

I often marvel at God's awesome power to shape my life by continuing to send people and events into my life to show me how much He cares for me personally. I also marvel at how dumb I have been on so many occasions by trying to take all the credit myself. There have been many times that God could have totally given up on me, but He didn't—and I think that is a miracle in itself.

Reaching the conclusion that I should write a book about Connie Maxwell was again somewhat of a miracle. It had been on my mind for a number of years but somehow I felt the timing was not right. I kept putting it way back in my mind. Finally one day I realized that I must make a decision - abandon the idea or give in and start writing.

Five of my mentors are Scott James, Harold Diggers, Mack Baltzegar, Dean Mahaffey, and John Sheriff with whom I consistently consulted in regards to this book. They prodded me, they cajoled me, they encouraged me, and they helped me.

They also wrote their life stories for this book. You will find them fascinating, enlightening, and inspirational as you read about them in later chapters of this book. Mack, Scott, John, Dean and Harold, like so many Connie Maxwell "kids," have been tested by fire and emerged winners. I only regret that I could not write about and publish all the stories that were passed along to me regarding "this Connie Maxwell story." To those of you who responded to my questionnaire I say, "THANK YOU a thousand times over. You helped me, you inspired me, and you made me grow. Every single story I read made me feel a deeper faith, a greater love for each of you, and a deeper conviction that Connie Maxwell has positively shaped so many lives. Every questionnaire that was returned to me made me realize that God was working in your life and mine even when we didn't know or realize that He was there. It made me think about the song, "*He Was There All The Time*." Thank you again for the time and effort you spent in responding to me. This book is truly our story, not my story."

A child has the uncanny ability of knowing when someone cares for and loves them and when they don't. (I don't know where this "knowing" comes from but I know it exists.) I think that is the reason we "Connie Maxwell" kids were so sensitive to some cottage parents. They were the only adult lifelines we had on a daily basis. We knew almost instantly if we were on the same "wave length" with them.

One cottage mother that helped shape my life was Mrs. "Hon" Gosnell. To me she was the same thing as "mom." Since my biological mother had died several years earlier, I was especially sensitive to having a "mother" in my life. "Hon" was a jewel. I don't believe I have ever met a lady that had the ability to say no and make you like it. She had such a soft voice, but when she said "no," it was "no." She didn't threaten, she didn't intimidate and she didn't push you. She was always there when you needed her. I regret to this day that I didn't tell her how much she meant to me before she died. I learned an important lesson from that experience. I am constantly examining those in my life that had a very positive influence on me. I either write to them or tell them in person what they mean to me.

I am not sure why I wanted to go to college when I left Connie Maxwell, but I was sure that I wanted to go. "Dr. Sam" encouraged me to go to North Greenville Junior College in Tigerville, South Carolina (now known as North Greenville College.) It was another positive move in my life in which "Dr. Sam" played a major part. He said he would see that Connie Maxwell paid for my tuition. I would have to pay for all my clothes, books, entertainment, and other incidentals. I was at North Greenville from 1954 through May of 1956. I graduated with an Associate of Arts Degree in May of 1956.

"Dr. Sam" said I could pay back my tuition to Connie Maxwell any way that I felt most appropriate. So in the summer of

1956, I started paying back twenty-five dollars a month. I thought it would take me forever to pay it all back. I finally did pay off the complete loan and I don't believe I'll ever forget the letter "Dr. Sam" wrote to me about how pleased he was that I had paid it off in its entirety.

It is amazing, as I write this book in August of 2000, how much I realize the responsibility I feel to imitate "Dr. Sam." I search out and look for those I can encourage, nudge or "stroke" to accomplish things they thought they never could—all because "Dr. Sam" never stopped doing that for me.

Every Christmas "Dr. Sam" would get me a job at the Greenwood Post Office. When college was not in session, all of us who were on campus at North Greenville had to leave to go home. I didn't have a home to go to so I went back to my real home where I felt needed, loved, and wanted -- Connie Maxwell. I stayed on campus for about two to three weeks every Christmas and walked back and forth to the old Greenwood Post Office to work. Christmas was a particularly busy time with a lot of mail to be delivered and so the Post Office hired "fill ins" to help the regular mail carriers. I have often wondered how many hundreds of contacts and phone calls "Dr. Sam" made for all of his "boys and girls" for situations just like mine. I will never know, but one thing I am sure of, he provided an example for hundreds of young boys and girls (including me) to follow that literally changed our lives. That is one of the main reasons I am proud to say I feel good about imitating him today.

I hope I will be able to expand on some of these thoughts in Chapter 7 entitled "*Staff - What Part Do They Play?*"

I didn't know what I wanted to do when I graduated from North Greenville College. I applied to a Baptist college in Jefferson City, Tennessee and was accepted. But I changed my mind in June of 1956 and decided to go to California to work in an aircraft factory in the little town of Palmdale, California. My brother was working for Convair Aircraft Company as a control tower operator at that time. I left South Carolina to seek my fortune in the great state of California. I was a dispatcher for electronic parts. My life away from school and a very protected environment had finally begun. I was like a young colt put out to pasture. I was foot loose and fancy-free.

I lived with my brother for about six weeks and then moved into an apartment of my own. I bought an automobile, was drawing a big paycheck every two weeks, and, for the first time in my life, had money to "throw away." I thought to myself "this is the place from where I will run the universe." Looking back on all of this I realize that ignorance and bliss are most definitely first cousins to each other. I stayed in California for a year and in May of 1957, I received a nice letter from the President of the United States, Dwight Eisenhower. He wanted two years of my life to be served in the U. S. Army. I was drafted and spent two years at various army bases in the southeast. Finally I wound up at Fort McClellan, Alabama in the chemical corp as a troop information officer.

I look back on my army experience as I have many other experiences in my life—I wouldn't take a million dollars for it, but wouldn't do it again for a million dollars either. You meet people from every conceivable walk in life—some of them share your philosophy about life and some do not. Some people will use you and sell you a "bill of goods" in a heartbeat. Some will reach out with time, encouragement, and help. My army career was definitely an eye opening experience.

It was also a time when I learned about a celebrity named Elvis Presley. I typed his discharge papers when I was on active duty in Atlanta, Georgia at Twelfth Army Headquarters in 1961. I felt I had a lot in common with Elvis. He was born January 10, 1935—I was born December 29, 1934 — thirteen days apart. Elvis was a very interesting and caring individual. He was born in poverty and was a very underprivileged young boy. He learned to play the guitar at the age of twelve and said he did so to escape and get away from his early childhood problems. I was so distraught when I first came to Connie Maxwell that I retreated inside myself and in the process learned to play the harmonica. It brought me much satisfaction in my early childhood. I still remember the pleasure of that early childhood experience.

I would like to close this chapter with an anonymous *"AN ODE TO SUCCESS"* I ran across many years ago. It reminds me of how many times I wanted to quit but somehow I kept going.

AN ODE TO SUCCESS

Perhaps there should be a point in our working life where we feel our contributions have been such that we are entitled to take it easy from that point on.

Maybe there should be, but we doubt it. The minute we start to relax on the oars, we begin to lose our value. Someone else, with more drive and ambition, could step in and do a better job in our place.

Let's face it, what we accomplished yesterday is water over the dam. More important is what we can do today and tomorrow.

When the things we did yesterday and last year are more important than our ambitions for tomorrow and next year, it is time to let someone else takeover.

This may seem like a hard, unfeeling way to look at things, but isn't it the truth? You can't win today's game on last week's press clippings. No success is final...no success lasts forever.

People who enjoy success have to plan to keep on succeeding. As each goal is achieved, they must look for a new one and keep on scrambling. That's what keeps life interesting!

When you feel you've "got it made", watch out! It's the first step towards settling back into a pleasant and convenient rut. People who have it made are only one step away from has-beens!

--Author Unknown

AND REMEMBER,

IF IT
IS TO BE,
IT IS
UP TO ME

"A generous man will prosper; he who refreshes others
will himself be refreshed." Proverbs 11:25 NIV

"Brethren, I do not count myself to have apprehended; but one thing I do, forgetting those things where are behind and reaching forward to those things which are ahead."

Philippians 3:13 NKJV

WHAT HAPPENED TO THE JAMES FAMILY?

Chapter 2

Understand that happiness is not based on possessions, power, or prestige, but on relationships with people you love and respect.

My father, Johnny E. James, was born at home in a rural section of Richland County in 1915, the oldest son of John Bunyon James and Hattie Caroline McPherson James. He lived all his life in this rural setting and probably did not finish school. During the depression of the 1930's my dad, along with a lot of other "under-employed" people, had to turn to the government for help. My father became a member of the "CCC" (Civilian Conservation Corp) doing anything the government wanted to help keep him, and others like him, employed, while at the same time, improving America in a variety of ways. While working on a CCC project in Barnwell County, SC in the late 1930's, he met Eloise Norris, a rural farm girl who eventually became his wife and my mother.

My mother was one of five girls born into the family of "Colonel" Benjamin & Cicero Norris. Sometime during the mid 1930's, a measles epidemic came through that area and killed my mother's mother, father, and baby sister, all within eight days. The four remaining girls, all in their late teens and early twenties, had the responsibility of taking care of the farm. It was an almost impossible task, even for experienced men. Probably out of desperation more so than love, all four girls ended up getting married. My mother was five years older than my father was. At no time during her life did she ever reveal this fact. Even her tombstone has the wrong birth date recorded on it so no one would know she had married a man younger than herself.

My mother and father settled in the Eastover community of Richland County and started to raise a family. On October 6, 1939, my older brother, Johnny Ephraim James was born. My birth (Wayne Scott James) was on January 30, 1942. My younger brother, Claude Blakely James, born on March 10, 1944. All three of us were born at home, delivered by a midwife or a family member.

We were a very poor country family who lived in a very small house that did not have electricity or running water. Our toilet was an out door privy located some distance from our house. Later on, we had a pump installed in our yard. We used kerosene lamps to light the house.

My father had a drinking problem, which caused him to be a very poor provider for his family. While Dad was well liked by everyone in the community, especially within his large extended family, he was not dependable and left a lot to be desired as a role model for his three boys. Dad worked his entire adult life as an automobile mechanic. All through my parent's marriage, my mother was by far, the stronger parent in every way. She struggled with Dad on a daily basis to get him to do the right thing from helping her with the kids, to bringing the check home to her instead of drinking it up with his friends, to keeping us in church each Sunday. With all the obstacles Dad put up, Mother was still able to save enough money to acquire a few acres of land located around the house where we lived. This land would play a major role later on in our survival.

Our home, as small as it was, was destroyed by fire in May 1946. The fire burned up everything we owned except the clothes we had on out backs. For the next couple of weeks, our family of five (mother, father and three young boys from ages two to six) lived in our barn which was not lost to the fire. We slept on corn shucks and covered with "croaker" sacks. Because the weather was pleasant, we did not suffer from the cold but we did have a lot of mosquito bites,

Less than a month after our home was destroyed by fire, father was critically injured in a one person, one car automobile accident. He ran off the road after coming down a long hill, was thrown from the car and was found a short time later. He had a severe injury to the back of his head. He was taken to the former Columbia Hospital in Columbia, SC where he died a day or so later. He was only thirty-one years of age, leaving his wife and three sons with no home, no belongings and no income. We were so poor that several family members shared the funeral expense.

We stayed with some of Dad's family for a short while after his death but my mother and Dad's family had a falling out, resulting in Mama having to move. Mother got some of her friends to build her a small shack, approximately ten feet square with a single door. She located it on my Dad's sister's (Eva Naomi James Wilson) property. We did not have any income and there was many a time when the only thing we had to eat was raw cow's milk, mixed with sugar and eaten with any bread we could find. Mother and Aunt Eva had a disagreement, resulting in mother having to move the small house we were living in. One of Dad's other sisters, Ola Mae Hinson, owned property a couple of hundred yards from where they were staying. Mother had some of her friends move the house. The way they did this was to cut pine trees into sections about twelve inches long. A cable was wrapped around the house and hooked to the back of a truck. The logs were placed in front of the small house so that the house was pulled off its foundation. The house would ride down the road on the logs to its new location. The house was located at the edge of a pasture and our only water supply came from a trickle of water that ran out of a bank nearby.

We were so poor that Mother and Aunt Ola Mae visited the Richland County Welfare office to see if Mother could get some type of relief so she could purchase food for the family. A temporary amount was awarded but we were never on welfare on a monthly basis. Things were very bad at the time we stayed at this location, which prompted Mother to try to rebuild on the site where our house had burned down several months earlier. As mentioned earlier, the land Mother had been able to purchase came in handy at this time. Mother sold some of the land she had purchased to get enough money to build a small house back at the old site. Once she did this, which took a short period of time, we moved back.

Just prior to the time our house burned down, Johnny had started going to school, Bellwood Elementary School, located near Hopkins, SC. Even though I was only four years old, Mother would send me to school with Johnny. As a result, when I turned five years of age, I started the first grade. The school we went to only had three rooms to handle seven grades. The first through third grades were housed in one room. There were six rows of seats, with two rows assigned to each grade. The teacher would work with one grade group for a while, give them something to do, while she moved to the next grade group, and so on throughout the day. The other two rooms had two grades housed in each one (fourth and fifth in one and sixth and seventh in the other). The teacher for the sixth and seventh grades also served as the principal for the school.

During the middle of my second grade year, things had become so bad that Mother moved us to Hartsville, SC (McFarland Street) to live with her sister, LaBelle and her husband, Howard Hopkins. They had two daughters, Kaye and Jewel, which were about the same age as Johnny and me. After Mother got a job with Hartsville Manufacturing Company she moved us about four houses down the street from where Aunt LaBelle and her family lived. The house we moved into was a flood zone, which caused the ground to become flooded each time it rained. All the houses had outdoor privies as well as open pits where water from sinks flowed. Of course, when it rained, all the waste flowed into people's yards, which created extremely unhealthy conditions for anyone living in the area. Shortly after we moved into the house, the local Health Department in Hartsville, found out the house was being rented and cited the owner for renting a house that really should have been condemned. The owner did not charge rent for a while until improvements had been made to the dwelling and surrounding area. From what I can recall, I can't remember any improvement ever being made except to have electricity installed. It was during this time that Mother sold the remaining land she had purchased prior to our home being burned. This small amount of money was able to keep us together as a family for a couple of years.

No matter what our family's condition, Mother always kept us in church. Even during the bleakest days after Dad's death, we

31

still went to church each Sunday. The same thing happened once we moved to Hartsville. We joined Emanuel Baptist Church located in the College Heights section of Hartsville. Preacher Little (I can't remember his first name) helped us immensely. We were very poor all during the time we lived in Hartsville. Because Mother had to leave for work before we had to leave for school and come home from work after school was out, she did not know we were starting to play "hooky" (skipping school). Johnny had good penmanship, even at that early age and he would write excuses for me to leave school early or to excuse my absences. Mother let Pastor Little know of our weak financial situation and the problems she was having with the three of us not going to school like we should. One time, Preacher Little called our family up before the entire congregation, informed the group of our plight, and asked those present to help us out financially. When we got home, I remember Mother being so happy when she counted the money and found around two hundred dollars had been given to us. This was a very big help for our family and helped us get over the next few months much easier than we had prior to this.

During the time mother worked for Hartsville Manufacturing Company, she met Mrs. Friedner, the mother of Jerry Friedner, a student at Connie Maxwell Children's Home. This meeting was a turning point in our lives. Because we were Baptists and Connie Maxwell Children's Home (Connie Maxwell) was a Baptist supported institution, Mother's eventual conversations with Preacher Little, resulted in a trip to Connie Maxwell in the summer of 1950. It was known in 1950 that something had to be done about our plight or we would end up as juvenile delinquents. Our future didn't look very bright. During this trip to Connie Maxwell in 1950, we met Superintendent Samuel M. Smith, later to be known as Dr.

32

Smith, who in turn introduced us to Jerry Friedner, a student at Memorial Cottage located near Dr. Smith's office. Dr. Smith, knowing we would probably be coming under the care of Connie Maxwell later on, tried to put us at ease as best he could by having someone from our home town show us around. That trip made a lasting positive impression in my mind and made our move to the campus the following year less painful.

My Connie Maxwell Years (1951-1959)

I can't remember very much about what went on just prior to our move to Connie Maxwell in the summer of 1951. But I do remember the tears shed by Mother in anticipation of the sorrow she would soon experience, and the tremendous support we received from our church family during that time. I remember clearly, the long ride, all 150 miles of it, from Hartsville to Greenwood, in the two black Cadillacs accompanied by Preacher Little and other church members. We arrived at Eastern Star Cottage, the most beautiful home on the Connie Maxwell campus. We were met by the cottage mother, Mrs. Mary Windham, who would be my guardian for the next couple of years of my life. After a short visit, Mother, along with Preacher Little and the others who accompanied us, got back in the cars and drove back to Hartsville. Needless to say, a lot of tears were shed that day. Mother told us she cried for days afterwards. She questioned herself as to whether or not she had done the right thing placing us at Connie Maxwell. She wondered what we would think of her later. We made sure she was reassured that she had done the correct thing. We loved her for the sacrifice she made in her own life to assure we had a chance to make a better life for ourselves than what she could provide for us.

33

Mrs. Windham tried to make things easy for us but all three of us boys cried numerous times over the next few days until we became accustomed to our new surroundings. Our transition was made easier knowing there was another set of brothers about our same age of us (Joe, Horace and Douglas Williamson) who lived in Eastern Star Cottage. Because so much of our free time was spent playing with the Williamsons, along with the other children in the home, we soon became accustomed to our new surroundings.

When I came to Connie Maxwell, my mother had already established my value system and my direction in life. What Mrs. Windham got was a person eager to learn other things that life had to offer. The two biggest impacts Mrs. Windham had on my life were the consistent use of good manners and how to conduct myself in a formal dining setting. Each Sunday, she insisted on having a formal meal after church: white tablecloths, formal table setting, best of china and a full course meal. It was during these times that the "aristocratic southern lady" side of Mrs. Windham came out. She wanted the children charged to her to know how to conduct them selves in a formal dining and living situation. She had a profound impact on all of us, instilling or reinforcing important values and standards we would carry with us the rest of our lives.

Mrs. Windham retired a couple of years after we came there, and was replaced by Mrs. Maude B. Davis. Mrs. Davis, in a lot of ways, was a young Mrs. Windham. She was a strict disciplinarian who also possessed great knowledge about the way to conduct yourself in social situations. I have to admit that I never really loved either of these two matrons, but rather, I feared them because of the strict moral code they forced upon us. In other words, with so many children in the home (eighteen when I first went to Eastern Star Cottage), there was no time for individual attention to a child's needs.

The cottage we lived in had been built with funds donated by the Eastern Star Chapter of the Masonic Order in South Carolina. It was a magnificent building with the look of an old colonial home. The two acres of land provided plenty of play ground for the kids. The grassy lawn provided plenty of space for kids to expend their excess energy and to grow up learning how to create opportunities for staying busy and out of trouble. I'm sure the vast amount of play ground room, along with the woods for boys to play in and explore, did more than anything else to keep us of out of mischief, which means TROUBLE.

There were approximately twenty active homes on campus in the early fifties. Some homes held up to twenty-four or more children. Over the years since that period, homes have been reduced to no more than eight children per cottage. This lower number of children per home makes cottage life resemble a normal home in general.

My brother, Johnny, who was two years older than I, was the more aggressive one of us boys. He forged ahead in making things happen, which often times occurs with the older child. In his case, he became a little aggressive and at the end of his junior year of high school, Dr. Smith asked my mother to take him back into her home for the last year of formal schooling. My younger brother, Claude, stayed at Connie Maxwell until I left in 1959. Johnny had left home by that time and Dr. Smith asked Mother to see if she could now care for Claude.

After graduating from Greenwood High School in 1959, I was given a four-year scholarship, which I brought to USC in Columbia, where I enrolled in the summer of 1959. I was so immature and ill prepared for college life that I became discouraged and dropped out after less than a full semester. I tried to get a job, but due to my age (seventeen years old) and, more importantly, due to the fact I had not met my military obligation, no one would hire me. Finally, in January of 1960, I joined the US Army because it had the shortest obligation period, only three years. After training at Fort Jackson in Columbia and later at Fort Leonard Wood in Missouri, I was stationed at Fort Belvoir located in Northern Virginia about ten miles from Washington, DC. Because I had always been fascinated with heavy machinery, my work area while in the army was in heavy machinery. I spent eighteen months in the US before being ordered to go to Germany, where I spent the last eighteen months of my obligation to Uncle Sam. While I was there, the Berlin Crisis arose and Johnny, my older brother, was called into active service. He was stationed in France. One weekend, he and I got a chance to spend time together in Frankfort, Germany.

After spending three years in the Army, I was discharged and came back to Columbia, SC. I went to work with Argus Camera Company, working in the die casting department, where I stayed for one month. I left there and went to work with Mutual Finance Company where I worked for three years, rising to the position of branch manager in Chester, SC. I moved back to Columbia and went to work with Columbia Hospital (later renamed Richland Memorial Hospital and even later, the name was changed again to Palmetto Richland Memorial Hospital.) When I went to work for Columbia Hospital, segregation was still in effect in the hospital system.

Columbia Hospital was made up of two units – the white unit and the Negro unit. My first job with the hospital was working delinquent accounts for payment. After about three months working delinquent accounts, the manager of the Negro unit was fired and I was moved to take over as Director of the Business Office. After integration came into being in 1966, the white unit became the private patient hospital and the Negro hospital was changed to the staff unit, which was for patients who did not have private doctors. I remained Director of the Staff Unit until Richland Memorial Hospital was built and both units of Columbia Hospital were shut down.

When Columbia Hospital set up the clinic system for poor people, I was asked to remain as Director of the registration area. I did so for the three years it took to get a new clinic building built on campus at Richland Memorial Hospital. After a few years at the new clinic site, I was asked to take over the financial operation of the Emergency Room, where I worked for about seventeen years.

In 1994, I was ready to retire under the state retirement system, but was asked by the administration to take over the collection department as a result of a major scandal occurring in which hundreds of thousands of dollars had been stolen. I became Director in April of 1994 and rebuilt the unit into one of the crown jewels of the finance division. I decided to get out of management in 1998 and retired effective July 8, 1998. I was asked to come back in some capacity. I agreed to do so with the understanding that I would never have to hire, fire, and train or discipline employees ever again, nor would I ever be placed in a position where I had to worry about the "bottom line" finances of the hospital. Since I came back in this capacity on August 3, 1998, I have been able to work in an almost "stress free" environment, which should help me live a little longer that I would otherwise.

I met my first wife, Patricia Ann Gjerdingen, shortly after I came to work with Columbia Hospital. We were married four months and four days after our first date. Two years after we were married, our first child, Patricia Alice James, was born. Three years later, our second daughter, Amy Elizabeth James, was born. My wife at that time, was a buyer for Richland School District #1. After nine years of marriage, she decided to leave our marriage for a salesman she had met in the course of her work. They were married and moved to Atlanta, Georgia. In our divorce, the courts awarded her primary custody of both girls and they moved to Atlanta with their mother. Those were the hardest years of my life but I was determined I would keep in touch with my two girls and be the best father possible. I made a commitment to keep my girls the focal point of my life and was successful in that venture. Today I have a very good relationship with both girls.

A couple of years after I was divorced, I met my current wife, Joan Elizabeth McCoy. When we met, she had been separated from her first husband (he owned an insurance agency and had taken up company with his secretary) for about fifteen months. After her divorce was final, we were married and have been together for nineteen years.

There were a lot of positive experiences from my years at Connie Maxwell. Most were simple, ordinary experiences that at the time didn't mean that much. Some examples were: having a strong work ethic; becoming independent; learning to live on your own without the comfort of a family to support you each day; learning to get by on much less than other kids had

38

as far as money, clothes, and other material things are concerned; learning to bond with other kids in the same situation; developing a strong "us" and learning to cope in situations where others would fail; having a strong scouting program where boys could learn about nature and develop a strong appreciation for the out-of-doors; riding horses; tending cows and hogs; learning about vegetables and how a farm works; knowing about the different plants, grains, trees, bushes and vines and the role they play in our world…and the list goes on and on. Boys who left Connie Maxwell knew more about more different things than the average child who grew up in town. We found ways to keep busy and to enjoy the small pleasures we were given and didn't expect others to make everything "all right" for us.

One of my mentors was Mr. William Clyburn. I came under his spell when I became old enough to work outside the home, somewhere around my twelfth birthday. In the beginning of working "on the farm," we had to rotate back and forth between the beef/hog farm and the vegetable farm. Later on, we were allowed to choose which type of work we preferred. I chose the vegetable farm. Mr. Clyburn ("Mr. C") was an avid sportsman, especially with bird dogs and hunting. I had always had a natural love for the out-of-doors, so when I got the chance, I would go along with "Mr. C" when he was training his bird dogs and hunting quail. During my stay at Connie Maxwell, I was the only boy allowed to have a shotgun housed on campus. "Mr. C" agreed to keep it for me and whenever he could, he would take me hunting with him. I killed my first rabbit, squirrel, quail, dove and pigeon while under his supervision. He taught me gun safety and the proper care of guns and dogs. He also had two horses he kept housed at the vegetable farm (Gypsy and Tammy) which he would let us ride from time to time. Because "Mr. C" was so well known throughout the state for training horses and dogs, he had a lot of opportunities to train both for some of the most influential people in the region. W. W. (Hootie) Ingram, a very high ranking person in the banking business in this state now, was a person who went hunting with "Mr. C" when Hootie was a young man. Lots of local doctors and persons with extra dollars to spend would hire "Mr. C" to break horses for their children. "Mr. C" would allow us boys to work with the horses while they were being broken and tamed so they would be gentle with the children who would later own them.

<u>"Mr. C" was truly a "good" man in every sense of the word. He meant a lot to me and I have to say, in retrospect, I loved the man.</u>

After I left Connie Maxwell and had been working about twenty years, I learned "Mr. C" had a stroke and was in a local nursing home in Columbia, SC. I went to see him and found him paralyzed on one side. I would help him to do small things and just talk with him. At this time, his wife had already died. Shortly after I started seeing him, he developed a second stroke that paralyzed him completely. When I would go by to see him, I would spend even more time with him, reading his mail, going over magazine articles, catching him up on what was going on with Connie Maxwell alumni and just making small talk to keep him company. Even though he was completely paralyzed, he still had a good mind and could communicate with me with his eyes. His eyes seemed to be so sad, looking back to me. I remembered him as a strong man. It was difficult to now see him completely at the mercy of the nursing staff who had to tend to his every need and body function. His daughter, Peggy, moved him back to Camden shortly after that and mercifully, he passed away a few months later.

Avery Home, our scoutmaster, had a lasting impact on my life. He knew a lot about scouting and was instrumental in teaching a lot of boys all about the wonderful world of scouting. The knowledge and skills he instilled in us allowed our scout troop, #52, to consistently out-perform all the other troops we competed against.

Some things that happened to me that helped bring success later on.

<u>The strong work ethic that was instilled in us at Connie Maxwell Children's Home helped me immensely</u>. I became a success due to hard work and long hours at the hospital where I worked for over thirty-four years before I retired. I worked with a lot of people who were smarter than me but I got ahead because I was not afraid of work and would stay with a task until it was successfully resolved.

I learned not to complain and to follow orders while at Connie Maxwell Children's Home. I was also in good shape physically. Once I left Connie Maxwell Children's Home and went into the military (three years in the Army), I was able to withstand the rigorous training and stay out of trouble. My three years in the Army were a success. I took this additional experience and carried it over into my civilian job (with the hospital) which also added to my success in my profession.

Because I came from a home with one parent and grew up around so many children from broken homes, I made a vow not to drink and to be a devoted family man. I have been successful in both of areas. After my divorce, my ex-wife took our daughters to another state. I made a concerted effort to talk with both daughters by phone every single weekend while they were away, and I would get them as often as quality time would permit. This effort paid off handsomely in the long run because one daughter elected to come live with me in her junior year in high school and both daughters treated me as their primary parent because of the dedication I had to them during their formative years. Because I knew the value of a college education in order to get ahead in this world, I instilled in my children's heads from early on that they would go to college. Both did, they graduated and both are successful in their career fields (one is a nurse with a business degree and the other is a psychology major working in graphic art design.) Over all those years of being away from me physically, I would not let them get away from me psychologically, and this bond grew stronger over the years. They came to realize the sacrifice I made, both monetarily and emotionally, so that we would stay in touch as a family. Knowing what other children have had to experience, from what I saw while at Connie Maxwell, I resolved I was not going to be responsible for causing my children to be scarred like that and, "thank goodness," they weren't.

I grew up to a lanky six foot while at Connie Maxwell Children's Home but weighed only about 150 pounds. I played basketball and baseball. I didn't go out for competitive sports until I was in the eleventh grade because I was shy and didn't want any attention drawn to me. I was a reasonably good athlete and could be counted on to be an asset to any team. Because the campus had become depleted of larger boys by the time I became a junior, I was almost forced to play. Once I started playing, I found I could be my natural self and stand up to the pressures of having attention directed toward me. This budding self-confidence allowed me to start dating and to become more of a social animal than I had been before. My last two years at Connie Maxwell were the most rewarding of the eight plus years I lived there. I had to be depended upon more and more by administration to take on responsible roles for Connie Maxwell (such as being the bus driver for school routes and campus activities.) I was left in charge of the vegetable farm whenever Mr. Clyburn was away. This added responsibility made me grow as a young man.

Once I got out into the real world after graduation from high school, the confidence I had started building carried me through. My social skills were still rather shallow but over time, I grew in the ways men and women interact with each other until I became just one of the group.

It should be noted that a large number of our boys played football for Greenwood High School during the fifties and sixties. Some were the stars of the team. Also, there were a few of the Connie Maxwell girls who were elected class beauty. If allowed to participate fully in school activities, Connie Maxwell kids were equally as bright, athletically gifted, and just as pretty as other kids who attended public school were.

My free time was spent in the woods. I loved nature in every way. I would make sling shots out of a branch of a dogwood tree and some book binder rubber bands I would buy at the local bookstore in Greenwood from money I saved by working Saturday afternoons (one dollar per month).

We didn't have much money to go to movies, but occasionally, I would go if a particularly good "action" movie were playing.

Back in the fifties, you could make an afternoon in town with just a quarter.

A movie cost nine cents, a coke was five cents, and a bag of popcorn was ten cents. That left us with one cent that we would spend on a penny piece of bubble gum to chew as we walked back to the campus.

How are things I learned at Connie Maxwell still shaping my life?

The biggest thing that my experiences at Connie Maxwell impacted on my life was the way I raised my children. Not only did I impose my work ethic, values, church commitment, discipline and appearance on the way I expected my children to be raised; I expected them to find value in what I imparted to them. In fact, my stepdaughter, who was the most trying of the four children in my life, now insists she will raise her children the same way I raised her. She has joked many a time that if her children ever give her trouble, she will send them to live with me so I can "straighten them up" for her.

What advise would I have for children at Connie Maxwell in the year 2000?

Listen to the advice given by the current staff and obey this advice. The world you will be going into is highly competitive and you need to be better prepared than I was in order to succeed. Study hard, take strong core courses, and participate in classroom activities. Develop a strong sense of self worth and confidence. Work hard to overcome shyness and other forms of self-doubt. Know you are just as good as anyone else. Be a good citizen. Problems are not solved with fists, knives or guns. <u>Walk away from trouble</u>. It takes a real man/woman to be able to turn away and not feel like your man/womanhood has been threatened. Staying in church when you leave Connie Maxwell will help you the most. Choose your friends wisely. Good friends will keep you out of trouble and will be an immense help when you are in need.

Why do some make it and some don't after leaving Connie Maxwell?

I believe this has a lot to do with the student's mental stability, family support after leaving, or support given by the institution when a student doesn't have a family structure to fall back on. If a person has pride, I believe it carries over into the challenges they face later on in life.

One of my best friends while I was at Connie Maxwell was "Mr. Everything" when he was in high school – star football player, good looking and had any girl he wanted, and voted Mr. Emerald in his senior year of high school. He had a childhood rooted in mental health problems and this overwhelmed him in his adult life. He married, had two kids, and was later divorced by his wife. He was crushed by all of this and was never able to overcome the situation. He currently works at minimum wage and doesn't have a cent to his name.

Why do some students make themselves out to be victims and not survivors?

I believe this happens when the student has low self-esteem. There is also a degree of shame associated with being brought up in an "orphanage" and some people use this to gain sympathy or to excuse away their failure in life.

I believe kids who left Connie Maxwell in later years (after I left) were better prepared to meet the challenges of the outside world because the staff on campus is better trained to help students learn the coping skills they will need when they leave Connie Maxwell. On the other hand, I believe students who left before my time, were less prepared to cope, which had a lot to do with the lack of training by staff, because times where less complicated during and before my time. Most students seemed able to succeed without the help students of today receive.

I left Eastern Star Cottage just before my senior year at Connie Maxwell and moved to Smith Cottage. There was something about its mystique that intrigued me. This was the cottage where all the big boys lived during my early years at Connie Maxwell. I roomed with Ed Sheriff and we became close friends. He had been a classmate of mine in the fifth grade.

The Dunbarton Infirmary was built from funds donated by a church in the small town of Dunbarton, SC. This is also the cottage where Bobbie Jean Emery lived. She was my first real love interest. She came to Connie Maxwell in early 1959 and we became each other's true love over the next few years. That deep abiding interest remains to this day. When Bobbie and I were dating, the rules stated the date would start at 7:00 p.m. and end at 9:00 p.m., sharp. Once, her matron, Mrs. Davis, caught us kissing and made me go home early. A few days later, in church, I got mad at Mrs. Davis and said some unkind things to her. Everyone in the church heard the commotion because I said it out loud at a time in the service when everything was as quiet as a mouse. I had to go back and apologize to Mrs. Davis before I could date Bobbie again.

Two particular occurrences come to mind that deserves remembering. The first time was when several of us boys at Eastern Star tied some sheets together and slid down them one night so we could go frog gigging at one of the local ponds on campus. We stayed out all night and didn't get a single frog. The next day when we were discussing this with friends, we finally realized why we didn't see any frogs. We had gone out during the wintertime when frogs were hibernating.

The other was when Lane Looper, along with another person whose name I don't recall, and I slipped out to go into town to attend a drive-in movie. During the show, they had a contest where you could win some money. I won twenty-five dollars that night and was so excited learning I had won that I gave the people my name, which was announced over the public address system. In church the next day, one of my classmates, Carolyn McCrory, came up to me and said she knew where I had been the preceding night. My blood started to run cold with the thought she was going to turn me in. When I learned she didn't have permission to be off campus either I was greatly relieved.

We were obligated to attend church and participate in all religious activities. As a child, this didn't have much interest to us but when we got up into our teenage years, we discovered girls and we tried to go to as many events as we could. In addition to Sunday morning church, Sunday school, Sunday night church and Wednesday night prayer meeting, there was training union meeting before church on Sunday nights that offered more of a social gathering than a church meeting. We used these opportunities to socialize with the opposite sex.

When I first went to Connie Maxwell, each boy's cottage had two older girls assigned to help with housework. One of these girls would be assigned to the kitchen and the other to laundry and housework. This was hard work for these girls, taking care of eighteen boys, one matron and the two of them. Boys who were too small to work on the farm were assigned to help these girls with the chores around the house. All this changed in the fifties when girls were no longer assigned to boys' cottages. Administration started hiring older ladies to manage the kitchens and the matron would manage the housework. An older girl from a girl's cottage would be assigned to work a few hours each day in the boys' cottage, helping the matron with laundry duties, etc.

There were several bad accidents that occurred on campus while I was there. The worst was the drowning of Tracy Leverette in the spring of 1959. Tracy had lived on campus for a few years and had returned to live with his parents in 1958. He was home less than a year when he was returned to Connie Maxwell. He had been back on campus less than two weeks when he and a couple of other boys went swimming in one of the ponds and he drowned. His body wasn't recovered until a day later. It was a very sad day for all of us.

While I was at Connie Maxwell, M. J. Rhodes was the beef and hog farm manager. He was a "man's man" in every sense. He was smart, well educated, hard working and strong as an ox. He required his men and students to work the full time they were assigned to him. After a while, the boys who worked for him dedicated a song out of the Baptist Hymnal to him – the song: *"Work For The Night Is Coming."* When Mr. Rhodes heard the boys singing that song, if he had had a bad day, he would scold the boys. In the eight years I lived at Connie

Maxwell, not one time did I ever hear of any of the farm managers hitting one of the students. They would punish the students but never hit them.

Mr. Blackwell and his wife were both raised at Connie Maxwell and were later married. He became a member of the staff and worked as head of the store room and cold storage freezer plant area for several decades. The Blackwells had two children, Clarence (the older child) and Millie (their daughter). During the summer when corn was big enough to can, all the students would gather at the old lunch room and clean corn so it could be taken off the cob and frozen for later use. In a lot of ways, this gathering was a social event in that boys and girls were able to work in mixed groups.

The beautiful gym we had was used for many years for a variety of functions. Basketball was the primary sport played in the gym. In the front entrance of the gym, was a wall dedicated to displaying team pictures and sports trophies. The pictures themselves were priceless. Sometime around the seventies, the gym burned down.

The campus had a grammar school that taught grades one through seven and after that, students had to go to public schools in Greenwood. I don't know how it was before the fifties but when I went to Connie Maxwell, I was a fifth grader and attended only one year on campus. Four from our class, two boys and two girls were selected to attend the sixth and seventh grades in a public school in Greenwood. I believe this had been going on for some time before my time. From what I was told at the time, this gradual weaning of students into the public school system was the prelude of things that were to come. After a few years of this, the higher grades on campus were slowly eliminated until finally all students now attend public schools. The old school house, which was located adjacent to the gymnasium, was not damaged when the gym burned down. In the early eighties, the school, which had been abandoned for years at that time, was finally torn down.

The alumni reunions are a highlight at Connie Maxwell. For years, reunions were held every four years. In the late fifties or early sixties, this was changed so that now, reunions are held every two years, the weekend prior to Father's Day in June.

-----Scott James

Author's commentary: As of May 2000, Scott James is still doing and giving of himself to his <u>family</u>, his <u>church</u>, his <u>community</u> and his <u>company</u>. His life is a monument to Connie Maxwell. I have lunch with Scott several times a year. I always come away with a renewed feeling of his being such an outstanding example of what Connie Maxwell is all about. I doubt I could say it any better than the following from an anonymous quotation entitled "_Resolutions_" – It reminds me so much of Scott and his life.

Resolutions

No one will ever get out of this world alive.
Resolve, therefore, to maintain a sense of values.
Take care of yourself.
Good health is everyone's major source of wealth;
With out it, happiness is almost impossible.

Resolve to be cheerful and helpful.

People will repay you in kind.
Avoid angry, abrasive persons; they are generally vengeful.
Avoid zealots; they are generally humorless.
Resolve to listen more and talk less.
No one ever learns anything by talking.
Be chary of giving advice.
Wise men don't need it and fools won't heed it.

Resolve to be tender with the young, compassionate
With the aged, sympathetic with the striving, and
Tolerant of the weak and wrong. Sometime in life you will have
Been all of these.

Do not equate money with success. There are many
Successful moneymakers who are miserable failures as human
Beings. What counts most about success
Is how a man achieves it.

                                                    --Anonymous

AND REMEMBER,

IF IT
IS TO BE,
IT IS
UP TO ME

"Train up a child in the way he should go, and when he
is old he will not turn from it." Proverbs 22:6 NIV

**"The Lord is near to all who call upon Him,
to all who call upon Him in truth."**

Psalm 145:18 NKJV

WHAT HAPPENED TO THE BALTZEGAR FAMILY?

Chapter 3

"No man is free who has not mastered himself."

I came to Connie Maxwell in March of 1941 with my two sisters, Bobbie and Millie. Bobbie was seven, Millie was four, and I was six. My mother was divorced and had three children. We lived in Orangeburg, South Carolina with my grandmother and her two children who were my mother's half brother and half sister. Mother worked in a sewing machine plant. It was very hard on her because she didn't make a lot of money. Times were hard. One day the pastor of her church in Orangeburg mentioned Connie Maxwell to her. Mother inquired and got in touch with Connie Maxwell. One of the social workers came and met with her. It's kind of history that my two sisters and I came to Connie Maxwell that March of 1941. I do recall mother saying that she did receive AFDC (Aid for Families of Dependent Children - a new federal program at that time.)

I remember the trip coming to Connie Maxwell but other than that I don't remember a whole lot about the first week or two at Connie Maxwell. I know we went to the sanitarium where we stayed for few days. Then Bobbie and Millie were sent to Children's Cottage and I went to Terrill Smith Home which was number five. I remember getting into a fight the first day that I was there. One of the boys tried to take some of the toys that I brought with me. I didn't like that so we got into a fight. That was one of the first experiences I had of trying to take care of myself. There were about twenty-five boys in our cottage ranging from ages eighteen down to six. I was six and one of the youngest boys in the cottage. We had our chores to do. We had to scrub the steps and the beds had to be made each morning. Some of us worked in the kitchen cleaning up the dishes and setting tables. The furnace and the wood stove had to be fired up each morning. There was a lot of yard work to be done. We had to sweep the yard with a broom that was made out of straw. In the early years that I was there, we were not paid. I am not sure what year we started receiving an "allowance." I first slept in an open-air ward where there were maybe twelve beds. We had big canvas rollers that rolled down to cover the windows. Each room in the house, I'm speaking of the ones that I stayed in the early years, had what we called a pig bucket. It would be put in the middle of the room. If you had to go to the bathroom you couldn't go downstairs at night; you would have to use the bucket. Of course, nobody hit the bucket and there was a mess every morning. Some body had to clean it up and that was also one of our duties.

We had study halls in the afternoon after we got home. We had to study for school and on Sundays we always had quiet hour. After we got back from lunch, we had to lie down for two hours whether you slept or not. There were a lot of times in the summer when we rolled up newspapers and had to kill flies. Sometimes this was done for punishment when we did something wrong. There was always a lot of glass around the yards. I remember one occasion that we had a glass roundup. We had to throw all the jars out of the attic and the truck came around and collected the glass. It was taken over to Laurens, SC to the glass factory.

We had a big bathroom that had two showers and three toilets with lockers around the walls. I remember the towel situation was horrible. There weren't enough towels to go around. Seems like they had two or three towels and they were always dirty. I usually would dry off with my clothes. The toilets seemed like they were stopped up all of the time. You had no privacy at all. That was some of the things you had to put up with, but we got through it all right.

In the basement of the house there was a furnace into which you had to shovel big lump coal. It would fire up and make steam that would heat the water for the radiators which heated the house. Later on we got a hopper that fed the coal right into the furnace. Sometimes the hopper would get stopped up but that was a lot better than having to shovel coal into the furnace.

We always had somebody to play with (twenty-five people in the cottage). We had enough to play any kind of game you wanted, whether it was softball, football or whatever. I remember my last two years there I roomed with another person (Bob McGill). We had two cottage mothers when I was there. Ms. Pratt was the first cottage mother and then Ms. Dillard came later.

On Saturdays we would go to town to the movies and we would have to walk. Some even hitched a ride on the train. We played on the railroad track. We would put pennies on the track. Once I saw some of the boys put grease on the track to see the train spin its wheels. We would play on the banks of the track using cardboard to slide down the incline. We would play in the woods just behind the barn that was known as the horse pasture. We built tree houses. There was a huge wide ditch between number five and number six where we often played. We would make kites. We would get sticks out of the fields and find string and using glue paste and newspapers, we made some really great kites. I especially remember we had kite contests and prizes for the best decorated kite.

Connie Maxwell had a mountain cabin and each cottage went up during the summer for one week. We would swim in the lake, eat goodies, play in the river and go on hikes. We surely had a big time at the mountain cabin. We would take trips to the high school during football season and American Legion in the summertime to watch the ball games that the high school played. Our clothes were not the best but they were adequate. There were church Sunday schools classes that would sponsor each one of us. They would send money and we would go get what we called "boxes." Basically we were required to go to church every Sunday morning for Sunday school and worship and on Sunday night we went to what they called BYPU. It was Baptist Young People Union where we learned a lot about missionaries and the Bible. Every Wednesday we attended prayer meeting. Benches in the church were real hard and on occasion some of the smaller boys would go to sleep and some body would pull their head up and drop it back. You could hear the noise pop all over the church. Dr. Murdock was always sitting at the front of the church and eyeballed everybody that was about to misbehave. I recall there were fans on the wall and you would count the rotations as they moved back and forth. Some were out of sequence and you would try in your mind to put them back in sequence. We had R.A.'s and G.A.'s and at times they would have pageants once a year that recognized the ones that had done well in both of these.

In Sunday school they had roll up doors that would separate each one of the Sunday school classes. In the summertime,

Dr. Murdock took the R.A.'s to Camp Rawls. There were contests and things in which I always did well. I was the star camper of the year a couple of summers. We had youth week at church where the youth took over all the responsibilities of the church services. One year I was youth pastor. I didn't really want to be youth pastor, but I did it and consider that as a good experience. We had a revival, I recall, when I was twelve years old. Rev. Arrington from Anderson was the preacher. He made such an impression with his sermons that I gave my heart to the Lord and I became a Christian. We had a very active choir where the girls and the boys could sing. I thought it was a real good choir. I didn't sing in the choir but my sister and Mildred, my wife did. They went to a state contest and did very well.

We had our own school on campus, grades one through seven. I remember very vividly walking from Terrill Smith, across the field and through the tunnel at the road. I once got into a fight in that tunnel. We would go to school and come back home and do our chores. We had our own lunchroom and while we were at school, we would march down to the lunchroom for lunch. Jack Herring, who was our football coach as well as our principal, would always have us sing a song "*When Jack Comes Marching Home Again.*" Assembly was used as a time for plays and activities put on by the students. On some Saturday nights movies were played in the gymnasium. We had to set up a lot of chairs; we all attended (the whole campus) and could see a movie. I vaguely remember one of the movies being *Westward Ho* or *The Way the West Was Won.* There was a bell on top of the school (I think that it's in the historical room now) that rang when it was time for us to go to school. There were declaration contests held at school. We had the opportunity to stand up and make a talk. I remember a May

Day Event with the flagpoles and girls dressed up in costumes. I recall field days once a year where we had the sack races and other games and races. You would grease up a pole, put something on top, (a prize) and then climb up and try to get it. After we finished the seventh grade, we went to high school at Greenwood. We would ride the bus each day. After we got back, we went straight to our campus homes. Our only contact with the town students was if they were in your class. Very seldom did I have any contact with anyone outside the school other than Rogers Cobb who lived in Greenwood. He got his mother to ask Connie Maxwell to let me come to his house on the weekend.

Judge Curtis Shaw's parents would ask Dr. Smith to let me come over to the Greenwood Mill and have dinner with them. I did that quite often and our relationship is still flourishing today. In fact, I went to Scotland with Curtis in the summer of 1999. We had a lot of boys and girls that would run for class office in high school and usually did well. We had students that would work in the high school dining hall and that was a way to earn extra money. If you worked in the dining hall you would also get to eat free. We were given every opportunity that one could possibly want in school. We had great teachers and they were interested in our welfare. They were interested in everything that we did and always encouraged us. When I was in high school some of the teachers had me to draw things for them. They acquired the materials for me and I would do the drawings. It was a good experience. We weren't able to socialize with the other students because we had to go home after school and work on the farm and on the diary. I had the opportunity to take piano lessons. I started the lessons but had a broken finger and the piano teacher asked me if I wanted to play the piano or play baseball, so I chose baseball. All the teachers, not only those at Connie Maxwell but also those in high school, did their very best to give us every opportunity and look out for our welfare. Dick Rhodes was in charge of the diary where we had milking cows. Later on it was beef cattle. Bill Clyburn had the vegetable farm where we grew vegetables. One of our chores was to take coal to the campus houses. Dick Rhodes had the responsibility of keeping all the grass cut around the campus. All of the bigger boys had to work on the dairy, the farm, the shop, or the print shop. The boys alternated between the farm and the dairy. I started on the dairy and after a short while, I decided I didn't particularly like that as much as working the farm, so I transferred to the farm. I worked for Mr. Clyburn most of the time. Dr. Sam offered me the opportunity of working at the print shop. To this day I regret that I didn't try because it would have been an asset to my art talents. Many times we would have to carry the milk cans around to the cottages when the truck broke down. We would have to pour half of it out because it was so heavy.

I remember when World War II was going on and at the end of the war German prisoners worked on our farm. They worked in the fields. Most of them had blonde hair. We were very curious about them. They were very nice to us. They couldn't speak our language but we seemed to get along okay with them.

We had to work the combine and tie up the grain sacks on the back of the combine. A lot of the boys wanted to drive the tractor. Some drove a tractor on Saturday afternoons and made ten cents an hour. One of our jobs was grazing the cows. At one time a lot of the cows got run over on the railroad track. That was a horrible sight. We had to clear land in the early fifties for pasture. We would dig up stumps, cut pulpwood, and unload car boxes. Particularly at Thanksgiving and Christmas, that was quite a chore. We would have to get the box cars unloaded within two or three days because the car boxes had to go back. They contained hay, loose corn, and some can goods. We used the corn and hay to feed the cattle during the winter.

One of our other chores was chopping wood. When it was raining and we didn't have a lot to do during the wintertime, we could chop wood. Another one of our chores was shoveling coal into the furnace hopper. We had to clean up the underbrush or hoe the strawberry fields or any crops that were growing at that particular time. During the spring, we planted sweet potatoes. We would get out school for a couple of days to plant sweet potatoes. We would carry water bucks to water the hole when we planted them. This would be an all day affair. In the fall we gathered the sweet potatoes. Then in the summer when the vegetables came in, we would gather them and take them around to the cottages. We would also have to take chickens to the cottages and ring their necks off for use on the weekend. Picking the okra was always a very itchy job. Peach farmers gave us a lot of peaches in the summertime.

In the early fifties we landscaped our whole campus and had to rake every inch of ground. We had to get all the rocks out of the soil before they could plant the seeds. We used a little push mower to cut the grass. It didn't have a motor on it; you had to push it. There wasn't much grass at first. But later on when the campus was landscaped, the grass came in and grew well, then we really had to cut the grass.

In sports, we had our own team on campus. Even though we went to high school, we had our own football team. It started out with a six-man team and eventually got into the regular 11-man football team. We played teams like Abbeville, Ware Shoals, Calhoun Falls, Lyman, Turkey Paw, McCormick, Edgefield and Ninety Six. These were the basic teams in our league. We would practice after work and usually we would have to practice by ourselves. Sometimes the coach wouldn't get there until we were about finished. We really wanted to play and we were disciplined enough to do the things that needed to be done, even if we did it by ourselves. We played on Thursday afternoons. Our uniforms were blue and gold. We had cheerleaders. We had a pretty successful football team. One year we only lost one game. I think that in my last year we lost only one or two games. We had our own baseball team and the teams that we played are the same ones that I just mentioned in addition to Greenville High and Anderson High which were two really big high schools. We didn't beat Greenville High but I know we beat Anderson High School. We had to practice after work on this, too, until it got dark. We always had big crowds at our football and baseball games and certainly our basketball games. Basketball wasn't as successful. Some how the other teams were a little bit stronger than we were. We had a girls team and a boys team. One of the big treats was when we would get to ride on the bus with the girls to the basketball games away from the campus. If you had a girlfriend you would get to sit with her. They had milk and sandwiches and usually the girls would give me most of their food.

We would practice after the girls' game. We had our own gym that burned down around 1970. The crowds were big and the gym was full with almost no available seating at our games. We charged for the basketball games. Bill McGill had a canteen that was between the gym and the school building. I ran it sometimes during the girls' game since they played first. We'd make a good bit of money. Bill played ball and, sometimes when I was not on the team in the early years, I ran it for him. Some of us were fortunate enough to play American Legion baseball – Nick Compton, Allison Gossett, Charlie Robinson, Grant Sullivan, David Robinson and myself. Every year we played, we went to the state championship. I know Charlie, David, Nick, and Allison were actually on the state championship team one year. The two years that I played, we played for the state championship but we didn't win either year. We played against guys such like Bill Dale who later played major league baseball and Bobby Richardson who was the star for the New York Yankees and Bill Christian who played for Detroit. We played against some good ball players.

I remember one time when I was playing high school baseball; I was late for practice. The coach suspended me from a game because I was playing marbles and failed to get to practice on time. Sometimes we would take a bike rim and get an old coat hanger and bend it just a little bit. We could go all over that campus for hours just rolling that bike rim.

I mentioned that we made kites and that was one of my favorite things to do. We made king kites and box kites and star kites and fish kites. I can still make them today. I remember one time, George Hunter ran for two hours with a kite. There wasn't any wind but he could keep it up in the air by just running around that big old field. We played touch football all the time. Each cottage had its own team. W also played among each other. We played baseball and softball in the yard. Everybody made a bow and arrow.

Everybody, including me had a sling shot. We played games like red rover and stoplight. The girls played jack stones and hop scotch. I remember we had what we called "a flying jenny." It was a board with a big hole in the top sitting on top of a post. We would put grease around it and you could get on the end and hold on while someone pushed you around. The flying jenny was a really a fun thing. We had two swimming pools. The first one was in front of the horse pasture. It was cold water that came out of an old artesian well. It was just a cement enclosure but it was where most of us learned to swim. Later, we had a new swimming pool behind the gymnasium. It was really nice and had a three-meter board. There we learned to dive and cut flips.

Connie Maxwell also had a social side. We would walk the girls home from the church. We dated in parlors. The girls would fix us something to eat. Sometimes it would be two or three couples dating in the same parlor. We would try to get in different corners so we could hold hands and maybe get a little kiss every once in a while. The cottage mother would keep walking by the door so that prohibited us from getting too close to one another. There were ball games and other activities that we went to at the high school. The boys went on the truck and the girls went on the bus. We would get with each other once we were there. We also had a junior-senior dance at school. I don't know how I had the money to buy clothes for the dance, but I had to go because I was the president of the senior class. We had Halloween parties where we would always have peanuts and cokes and play little games like spin the bottle. I would see my two sisters at church, and, on occasion, I would go down to their house to see them.

We had a chance to go home for Christmas. I really didn't like to go home at all because Connie Maxwell was my favorite place. I didn't feel that my stepfather wanted me at home. When I was there I felt uncomfortable. We had a chance to go home for a week in the summertime. I went for a number of years but when I had a chance not to go, I didn't. We had church socials frequently and sometimes we would go to the State Park where we could picnic and swim. I remember the Lion's Club would always sponsor us every year for an Easter egg hunt. We would go on the bus and some of us would get to go on the fire engine. They would turn us loose and we would hunt for Easter eggs. They would give us each a dime and then we would go to the movie.

We had the boy scouts. Not only the boys scouts but also the explorer scouts. The explorer scouts came after I left. In fact, I was the first explorer scout leader. The Jaycee's had the boy scouts and the explorer scouts. It was quite an adventure for us to be able to do things with the boy scouts. To be on your own and go to Camp Old Indian in the summertime in Greenville.

What has Connie Maxwell really meant to me? I don't have any way of knowing how I would have turned out had I not been raised at Connie Maxwell. One thing for sure, I did go to Connie Maxwell and my stay shaped my life from the very first day until the present day and will for the future. I learned very quickly that I had to take care of myself and grow up in a hurry. I had to take care of my own needs, my personal items such as clothes and what little money I had. I don't remember having very much at all. Things have changed quite a bit now, I understand. You had to be able to take care of what belonged to you because no body else would. I learned to be creative, especially in the games that we played. Connie Maxwell gave us a great opportunity to be creative. I learned to be responsible at any early age. I had my responsibilities to do in the morning before I went to school. I had to be responsible for my actions if I did something that "<u>broke the rules</u>." Not only if the cottage mother saw it but if the older boys saw it, I had to pay the consequences for what I did. My stay at Connie Maxwell offered me numerous opportunities. We had a chance to work on the farm and the dairy where animals were involved. We were taught how to care of them. We learned how to plant and harvest vegetables. We learned how to be part of team and to be a team player – not only at work but also in basketball, football and baseball. We learned how to drive tractors, trucks and buses. I even learned how to drive a car there - I got my license while I was at Connie Maxwell. We were offered every opportunity that young person could possible want and need in a lifetime. I was given the opportunity to get a college education. I had to pay half of it back – you borrowed the money you needed and you would pay half of it back after you graduated. I learned that someone cared about me and about my welfare and was always interested in what I was doing. Matrons or, cottage parents as they are called now, were always doing the best that they knew how for us even though there were twenty-five children in a cottage. I know they were spread thin and could pull their hair out with our antics, but they still were faithful to us. They were faithful not only to us but they were faithful to their Lord. Work supervisors made us work hard but they let us know there was a reason that we had to work. It was to help the home to have something to eat and to get by without having to hire other people to do the jobs that needed to be done. The home actually depended on us to work.

I can't say enough about how good the schoolteachers were to each one of us. They tried to do their best to provide us an excellent education. The social workers kept us informed about our families and our parents. The superintendent always talked to us and was always looking out for our best interest. He had us foremost in his heart at all times. There were two superintendents when I was there. Dr. Jamison was the first one. When I was old enough to get the mail, I would stop in his home and read the *New York Times*. He gave me the first waffle that I ever had. I will always remember him for thinking of me as an equal to him. He didn't try to act like he was any higher than I was. "Dr. Sam" was certainly one of us and looked out for our welfare at every turn.

Through the church I came to know there was somebody greater than myself. I learned about Jesus and how He died for my sins. I accepted Him as my Savior at the age of twelve. To this day, I hold Him as the mainstay in my life. This was an opportunity that was given to me over and over every time I went to church on Sundays and on Wednesdays. We learned about the Bible and the history of the Bible. I learned how to share and how to give and how to take and be responsible for myself. Each Thanksgiving and Christmas, churches all over the state would send us boxcars and trucks with goods for our livelihood. Special people would give us money to purchase clothes. I realized they gave because they had a love, not only for Connie Maxwell, but a love for the children at Connie Maxwell. It wasn't just a mission to them. They had a really special place in their hearts for Connie Maxwell. In fact, they had a special day that they gave – the fifth Sunday of the month was just for Connie Maxwell. I realized that I had a home with many brothers and sisters. All through my early years, this was extremely important. Today it remains as a place that I can always call home. I can always call on my brothers and sisters from Connie Maxwell any time there is a need.

I learned manners and especially how to say "Yes Ma'am" and "No Ma'am." I learned to respect others; to respect what they had – it belonged to them. I learned to have patience even if things were bad. I was taught from an early age that things would not always be rosy and you had to work for the things you wanted and needed. Many good people had an influence on my life there. I never went hungry or without clothes. There was always someone to play with or to listen to you when you needed it. The Bible became real to me and Jesus became my Savior. <u>I felt loved and secure there</u>. Connie Maxwell gave me a chance to grow up in a loving environment. I count my blessings each day that I was fortunate enough to have lived at Connie Maxwell.

I especially enjoy the alumni reunions every two years. The gathering of all the boys and girls that you grew up with and seeing some of the young folks that are there now and knowing they will be your brothers and sisters in a short time.

I left Connie Maxwell and went to Furman University and then into military service where I spent most of my time in San Antonio, Texas in the medical field hospital. While I was in service, I married Mildred Hair who was also raised at Connie Maxwell. We have two children, Star and George. After my military service we moved back to Greenwood. I lived on campus for about five years and helped with the boy scouts, did some campus work, and worked at the church. We took children in our home that were problem children until they found another place for them. Later we moved into

Greenwood, bought a house, and I worked at the YMCA. Later I worked at the two junior high schools and taught art and physical education. And, finally, I accepted a job at the vocational rehabilitation department and worked there for twenty plus years and retired in 1988. I have had my own art studio and frame shop since I retired. One of my sisters, Bobbie, lives in Greenville where she owns Greenville Printing Company. My younger sister, Millie, lives in Santa Ana, California where she enjoys her children and a wonderful family life. We all are very appreciative of the opportunity that mother gave us by realizing that Connie Maxwell would take us in and be our "mother." Connie Maxwell is a home that has a lot of love and a lot of dedicated people. Connie Maxwell is a place where you have an opportunity to make something out of yourself. It's a place where you are cared for and loved. Many people don't really know about Connie Maxwell, simply because they feel like it is something for juvenile delinquents. It's a place that offers love and care for children that are in need. <u>It's not only been in existence for the past one hundred and eight years, but it is available today for children in South Carolina who need care and nurturing. Probably as long as there is a world, there will be a Connie Maxwell to take care of children who are in need.</u>

----Mack Baltzegar

Author's commentary: I have known Mack since I was in the 6th grade. I have often wondered why I have looked up to him all these years. Now that I have read "his story," I know why. I asked the question at the very beginning of this book, "Why are some people tested by fire and come up winners and why do some fall apart at the seams under the same circumstances?" Mack is a winner because he held true to the ideals he learned at Connie Maxwell. And, Mack is a winner because of his love and commitment to Jesus Christ.

Mack loves to paint and draw. Several of his paintings are on the walls in our house and I have given a great many to friends all over the United States. I have told him on more than one occasion that he could have been a very, very famous artist.

Mack is a role model and someone to emulate. He sets an example for all of us to follow. I am thankful to call him my friend and my brother. I am thankful to let the world know that he is an alumnus of Connie Maxwell Children's Home.

AND REMEMBER,

**IF IT
IS TO BE,
IT IS
UP TO ME**

"I will not leave you as orphans, I will come to you."
John 14:18 NIV

"Great is our Lord, and mighty in power; His understanding is infinite."

Psalm 147:5 NKJV

IS BEING AN "ORPHAN" A PLUS OR A MINUS?

Chapter 4

Be bold and courageous. When you look back on your life, you'll regret the things you didn't do more than ones you did.

With great sorrow, comes great wisdom.

The first thing here is to define the term "orphan." Webster's unabridged dictionary says, "someone who has no mother or father living." Most of the children at Connie Maxwell were not "true" orphans according to this definition. The children on campus when I was there in the forties and the fifties were there for many different reasons – such as alcoholism, divorce, abandonment, or one or more parents deceased, committed to prison and/or mental hospital.

A number of children at Connie Maxwell were there because the surviving mother or father in the family desperately wanted to keep them, but simply could not economically do so. They knew they were loved but they also knew that they were not "living at home." Connie Maxwell became their home.

Then, we should define the word "orphanage." Webster's Unabridged Dictionary says, " a location where orphans are housed and kept." For those reading this, you may take offense at the words "housed" and "kept." I would say to you as a former student at Connie Maxwell, I did not feel "housed" or "kept." I don't believe there can ever be a place that can completely take the place of "home," but Connie Maxwell is as close as it can come. I felt like it was "home."

When Connie Maxwell was first founded by the South Carolina Baptist Convention in 1892, it was known as Connie Maxwell Orphanage.

In 1946 the convention realized that a name change was needed and it became known as Connie Maxwell Children's Home. The mission statement that is in effect today (2/1/2000) reads as follows:

MISSION STATEMENT

The purpose of Connie Maxwell Children's Home, a ministry of the Baptist people of South Carolina, is to enable children and families to improve their relationships and meet their needs in ways that are in keeping with the teachings of Jesus Christ.

This brings us back to the title of this chapter, *"Is Being An Orphan A Plus or A Minus."* I personally can attest to the fact that for me it is a plus. I am sure you could find some alumni from Connie Maxwell that will tell you some stories that are negative and will say it is a minus. I am also sure that you could find a number of people who were raised in a "normal" family that have had some bad or negative experiences in the process of "growing up." I commented in the very first chapter that anyone growing up, even in a normal situation, would have some things happen to them that could be considered negative or bad. Let me carry you on a short journey that will give you some reasons to understand why I say "my experiences growing up at Connie Maxwell and being an "orphan" was a plus – not a minus.

First, I was taken out of a home situation involving alcohol. I was not abused, molested, or beaten, but it was not a very good situation in which we three, my brother, my sister, and I lived.

Second, I was put into a situation that gave me shelter, love, clothes, support, a secular education, and, very importantly, a Christian education.

Third, I was encouraged to better myself by doing a number of extra curricular activities that helped me to build relationships with others.

Fourth, I was encouraged to play sports and learn sportsmanship and to be competitive but not to be aggressive. This concept leads me to "go the extra mile." Just being good enough is not good enough.

Fifth, I had an opportunity to be in the same situation with approximately 325 to 350 other children. I didn't feel different. We were all brothers and sisters to each other. I often say to other people that I have a world record. I have at least three hundred to three hundred fifty brothers and sisters that I love very much and who love me.

Sixth, Connie Maxwell has in place (and has had for quite a number of years) a plan whereby any student who graduates from high school can go on to college. The plan not only includes college but technical schools or other institutions of higher learning. Dr. Smith helped me and encouraged me to go to North Greenville College. It was a good decision on my part and with financial help from Connie Maxwell, I was able to graduate with an Associate of Arts degree in 1956.

I could probably think of another eight or ten reasons why "being an orphan" was a real plus for me. I will stop here with my personal reasons and go on to why "anyone" who is raised as an orphan should think of it as a positive experience and not a negative one.

I have known a number of people in my lifetime that was raised in an alcoholic family situation. Some of the things they have told me would make your toes curl up. I have seen families so torn apart that any possibility of ever getting that family back together was very, very remote. Connie Maxwell took me out of a similar, but not quite as bad, a situation.

Any young boy or girl who ever comes to Connie Maxwell comes there because of a bad home environment and/or some other similar situation. Before I started writing this book, I asked some twenty-five to forty former Connie Maxwell students to tell me their life's story. My heart went out to everyone who took the time to answer the eighteen questions I had provided. It was evident to me that almost all of them had suffered some very desperate circumstances in their lives, but every single one had considerably more good things to say than they had bad things to say about being at Connie Maxwell. Everyone who responded to my questionnaire felt the saying at the beginning of this chapter, "With great sorrow, comes great wisdom" was a good one – making lemonade out of the lemons they were given. I hope that you will pay special attention to chapter five, "*Adversity – A Stumbling Block or A Stepping Stone*" as we talk more about why some people handle adversity with tact and skill and just plain "guts" and others almost come part at the seams.

I mentioned earlier that I had at least three hundred to three hundred fifty brothers and sisters. Since Connie Maxwell took in Susie Burton from Newberry, SC, in May of 1892, there have been several thousand children who have come and gone through the doors at Connie Maxwell. Some came who were severely damaged before they ever arrived on campus and left adapted and ready to take on the world. Some others came under the same conditions and left bitter and angry.

"Is being raised an orphan a plus or a minus?" There will be some who will read this book and take serious issue with me regarding the use of the word "orphan" and "orphanage." Somewhere in the back of their mind they may be thinking about things they have seen or heard about war conditions or poverty or revolutions or natural disasters or other similar conditions. There have been some movies that depict terrible conditions for young boys and girls. These scenes almost make my emotions stand on end. My heart stops when I see a child that has no one to whom they can turn. My heart goes out to them in a way that makes me stop and consider their plight. It is almost as though they are at the mercy of the wind. These scenes would pull at your basic emotions and challenge your sense of fairness. The word "orphan" makes me feel like I was a helpless victim – carried by the tide of life with no real control over what was happening.

I have done a great deal of changing in the last two years since I started working on this book. I specifically and deliberately chose the word orphanage for five reasons.

Number One: I felt the need to capture the emotions and feelings of anyone that might see the title and wonder how it was to be raised in an orphanage.

Number Two: I hoped the title would be responsible for waking up someone who was raised in an orphanage or children's home and has felt like a victim of life and its circumstances. Perhaps it can help them break out of that mold and move on to bigger and better things.

Number Three: I felt the need to use the word in order to feel safe and secure in my own mind about how I personally felt about being raised in an orphanage.

Number Four: I felt the need to shake the belief once and for all that "orphans" need to be felt sorry for or treated differently than "normal" children.

On June 9-11, 2000, about five hundred other Connie Maxwell alumni and myself attended the reunion we have every two years on campus in Greenwood, SC. It was a time to hug, cry, kiss, reminisce, tell stories, and in general, remember our childhood at Connie Maxwell -- it literally was a "coming home time." I never go back that I don't feel that same level of security, safety, and love that lets me know "I am home again." It would be impossible to totally describe that feeling in detail. No matter what is going on in my life at the time, I still get this feeling that "I am home" again.

This feeling of security and safety came from the staff who helped us know we were loved and we could feel safe and secure. I plan to go into this in greater detail in chapter six, *"Staff - What Part Do They Play?"*

There is a little place inside all of us as human beings that should never be allowed to "grow up." I always get that little boy feeling when I return to campus. I hope I never lose it.

Another reason that being raised as an orphan was a plus for me always comes out in our trustee meetings at Connie Maxwell. I was elected Chairman of the Board of Trustees of Connie Maxwell in November of 1999 to serve during the year 2000. A lot of decisions I am asked to make directly reflect my time and experiences at Connie Maxwell.

One particular decision that brought me much anguish and, at the same time, much satisfaction, was serving on the "Land Use Task Force" in the winter of 1998. Dean Mahaffey, a dear friend and sister, and the Chairman of the Board of Trustees, at that time, asked several other trustees and me to serve on the "Land Use Task Force" committee.

It was a brand new committee that Dr. Jimmy McAdams and Dean had formed in order to examine and analyze the use of the land, property, and real estate that Connie Maxwell owned to determine if it is being used to its fullest and best advantage. The committee consisted of Jerry Friedner (chairman), Gene Bishop, Dean Mahaffey, Danny West and Danny Nicholson. We spent countless hours looking at and going over all the land owned by Connie Maxwell.

The committee realized that the farm operation had greatly decreased over the years and had not been profitable for sometime. About two hundred twenty-five acres on the west side of the Highway 25 bypass that runs through the Connie Maxwell property was not being used and had not been used for several years. The land was not needed as pasture, so it just lay there with no use and no expected use. All of the committee members agreed unanimously to make an effort to sell it. It was not part of the land that Dr. Maxwell gave to the South Carolina Baptist Convention in the early 1890's.

However, it was very close to my heart. I had worked countless hours along with a number of other Connie Maxwell students to clear it and make it usable as pasture. Part of me was still in that soil but I voted to sell it under some very strict guidelines regarding how it would be used. The one thing that clinched my vote was something that Dr. Jimmy McAdams said in one of our meetings, "How will selling this land impact our using the money for helping children in need in the tender ministry we are working so hard to provide,"

I thought of myself in 1947 when nobody wanted me; but Connie Maxwell said, "We will take Gene under our wing along with his brother and sister." There is no doubt in my mind that Connie Maxwell saved my life. I would today either be in the state penitentiary or dead. I tried a thousand times to put myself in the shoes of hurting children, and to this day, I have no regrets about selling that land. The one over-riding thought that came to my mind, was the impact it would have on children that were just like me - children who have no place to go and no one to take care of them or to give them the security, love and safety I was shown.

I would like to close this chapter by using a copyrighted "Essay" entitled, "*Here Comes The Dawn*."

HERE COMES THE DAWN

After a while you learn the subtle difference between holding
a hand and sharing a life.

And you learn that love doesn't mean possession and company
doesn't mean security and loneliness is universal.

And you learn that kisses aren't contracts and presents aren't
promises and you begin to accept your defeats with your head
up and your eyes open with the grace of commitment and
not the grief of a child.

And you learn to build your hope on today as the future has a
way of falling apart in mid-flight, because tomorrow's ground
can be too uncertain for plans.

Yet, each step taken in a new direction creates a path toward
the promise of a brighter dawn.

And you learn that even sunshine burns, if you get too much.
So you plant you own garden and nourish your own soul, <u>instead
of waiting on some one to bring you flowers.</u>

And you learn that love, true love always has joys and sorrows,
seems very present, yet is never quite the same – becoming
more than love and less than love – so difficult to define.

<u>And you learn that through it all you can really endure; that
you are really strong; that you have value; and you learn and
grow. With every good bye you learn</u>.

Copyrighted 1987 – Joy Whitman

AND REMEMBER,

IF IT
IS TO BE,
IT IS
UP TO ME

ADVERSITY: A STEPPING-STONE OR
A STUMBLING BLOCK?

Chapter 5

Smooth seas do not make skillful sailors.

Adversity introduces a man to himself.

I didn't realize how much I had let myself become a "victim" of circumstances until I listened to a series of audio tapes by M. Scott Peck entitled, *"The Road Less Traveled."* When we let ourselves become a victim we give almost unlimited power to everybody and everything except ourselves. When we let ourselves become powerless; every wind that comes along blows us about. Everything that happens to us becomes the fault of someone else and their responsibility. A number of things happen to us when we feel and act like a victim.

Number One: <u>We start feeling sorry for ourselves</u>. This attitude creates a feeling that I can and have been taken advantage of by others and by circumstances.

There are often very good reasons for our conflicts and differences with others. We need to be mature enough to pick our own conflicts, in our own time, and in our own way whenever this is possible. There are times and places when confrontation needs to be handled there and then. We don't always have the luxury of going away and feeling sorry for ourselves. Patience is a good thing to have but a bad thing to overuse. There are times when feeling sorry for oneself has some justification if we use it properly to reevaluate the facts of the situation. But to let this become a "normal" reaction to conflict, hurt and disappointment has a serious downside. The feeling that you have no control over the situation results in a high level of stress and anxiety. We need to raise our awareness level, so we can see how we are reacting and then pressure ourselves to not let it happen again.

Number Two: <u>We start blaming other people</u>. This attitude basically absolves us of any responsibility. Everything is always the fault of someone else. The thought that we could have caused it or prevented it or dealt with it differently does not even enter our mind. It robs us of any creativity to try something new or do something differently. We get the "why bother" feeling. When that prevails it leads to relationship failures because the people around you are forced to take the blame for your blunders or for what has happened to you.

Number Three: <u>We get the mind set that "we don't have to do anything."</u> This absolves us of any responsibility to correct the situation -- <u>"all blame, no gain."</u> If we challenge this attitude in ourselves, we grow; if we don't challenge it, we stagnate.

When we challenge this attitude in ourselves it may create conflict; and <u>not all conflict is bad</u>. Conflict, more often than not, will help clear the air, resolve the differences that have been smoldering. <u>Resolving conflict gives us confidence to handle the next conflict,</u> with the same person or situation or with something or someone new.

Number Four: <u>We get a feeling of "I don't have to change."</u> The one thing that you and I must do every day of our lives is change. Change is the one sure thing we can count on. Nobody likes to change. We all have our own "comfort zone" and we like to stay in it. Seeing ourselves as victims makes us feel we don't have to change.

Stress management trainers tell us that the two most common things that cause stress in our lives are <u>change</u> and <u>managing time</u>. We may never be perfect regarding these two things, but we need to increase our awareness level. We can easily become our own "victim" when we don't manage our stress and our time.

Number Five: <u>We decide, "I don't have to confront anybody."</u> This attitude may be the hardest to change. I very much dislike conflicts in any given situation. <u>A number of times when conflict has arisen in my life, I became nervous and got quiet and had a hard time "confronting" the person that caused the conflict.</u> We tend to lose some of our self-respect when we don't confront the person. We should use the type of judgment that lets us be appropriately confrontational but not overly aggressive or militant.

Number Six: <u>We decide, "I don't have to stand up for myself."</u> One of the things that build self-esteem is the ability to stand our ground when we know we are right.

My wife, Pat, and I facilitate the divorce recovery program at our church. The class consists of separated or divorced participants. A fairly consistent problem we observe has to do with the balance of power between the spouses. When one party has or exerts more power than they should the other party has a need to step in and create balance. In other words and in a non-aggressive manner, <u>"stand up for yourself."</u>

Number Seven: We act as if we can hold moral superiority over others. There are those people who wear their moral superiority like an award given at a big banquet. When someone feels like they are morally or ethically superior to others, they send the signal that they are "better" than the other person is. Just because someone has more education or is more gifted doesn't mean that individual is better, just that they are blessed in a different way. In other words – remember that all of us grow at different paces and have different talents. All of us have a lot to give to our families, our church or community and then back to ourselves.

I would like to go considerably deeper in explaining these seven statements and at the same time, share with you some surprising information and statistics from Dr. Richard McKenzie. I meet Dr. McKenzie in 1998. He is the author of an outstanding book entitled, *"Rethinking Orphanages for the 21st Century."* I will be quoting extensively in this chapter from his report drawn from his book, "Rethinking Orphanages for the 21st Century" - Sage Publications Inc.

To give you some idea of what I am trying to convey, I would like to quote from the foreword of Dr. McKenzie's report (written by Mitchell B. Pearlstein:)

"Yet while we are honored, we are also aware that any number of readers are primed to discount it because they simply cannot fathom that anything decent or uplifting can be said of a group home for kids, whether they're called orphanages or something more imaginative. I would urge such folks to dismiss not orphanages themselves, but the sorry, often

demagogic stab at a national debate on this abused subject several years ago." [1]

I hope that some of the information from this chapter will help create a different look at "foster homes" vs. "orphanages." We use the word "orphanage" herein when referring to orphanages, group homes, and children's homes.

In December of 1999, I was looking at a well known television program, "60 Minutes." Several million people saw the same program I saw that night about orphans and orphanages in Germany. The orphanage was being operated by a group of Catholic Nuns. The nuns were unquestionably mean and abusive to the boys and girls there. I personally felt sorry for the children but it made me think about myself and how I was raised and how different it was. I'm sure the program left many people very cold and very concerned about "orphans" and "orphanages."

I began gathering information in order to write this book by sending out a number of questionnaires to my friends (my brothers and sisters) who were raised at Connie Maxwell. I was amazed and delighted at how many said their experiences at Connie Maxwell were positive. I was struck by the feeling that living at an orphanage for them was like going to live in a palace compared to the conditions from which they came. I am sure that a big percentage of these children were saved from tragic circumstances by being removed from their "homes" and going to an "orphanage."

Looking back on the questionnaires I sent out, I am amazed and delighted at the number of alumni who have become outstanding mothers, fathers, and citizens of their communities, good community leaders, presidents of corporations, successful in many ways. And, there were some failures, but by far the children who were raised at Connie Maxwell turned out to be wholesome, good, responsible and successful people. I have no idea what the overall percentage might be regarding success vs. failure; but I can tell you this, the successes far outweigh the failures.

A permanent orphanage is a thousand times better than a terrible situation at home where neglect or sexual, physical, or emotional abuse or, even, violence is the order of the day.

Sometimes I am amazed at how and why we think a group home or children's home is worse than a home where the child is consistently abused or stands a chance of becoming a career criminal.

"Currently, children in foster care constitute less than .003 percent of the nation's population, (three one-hundreds of one percent), while 17 percent of state prisoners are former foster-care children, 40 percent of foster children leave the system to go on the nation's welfare rolls, and 39 percent of the homeless youth in Los Angeles County are former foster-care children.[7]" [2]

I am not writing this book to judge or put down the foster care system but I feel I would not be fulfilling my obligation to my fellow alumni and to children's homes in general if I did not point out some things that Dr. McKenzie uncovered.

"Judges and child-are workers across the country openly decry the fact that many abused and neglected children will be sent home from the foster-care system only to be abused again and returned to the system for another round of foster placements." [3]

Foster care and children's home alumni would be the first to say, let's work to change some things about the system. A great number of men and women should never have become a parent, but the mindset of the system is to return children to their biological parents. They often go back into the same terrible situation they came out of where the abuse and neglect continues and even becomes worse.

The mind set that foster homes are always better than orphanages or children's homes needs some serious rethinking. Some religious denominations are presently looking at building and staffing private orphanages. *"The Lutheran Churches of California project dubbed "20/20/20" plans to build twenty children's homes in twenty cities in twenty years. Children's homes that two and three decades ago became short term treatment centers are reconsidering their mission with an eye toward reintroducing long term residential care for children who are not able to return home or who would likely continue to move from one foster placement to the next."* [4]

"One child-care expert, whose authority is grounded in his professional work and his background as an orphanage alumnus, suggests that a good start for a child almost always encompasses four attributes: <u>connectedness, continuity, dignity, and opportunity.</u>

- By _connectedness_, he means that "children need to feel that someone is there for them, and that they are a part of someone else's life."
- _Continuity_ is "a sense of continuous belonging with another person or persons. The young person needs to feel a part of a greater whole and has an important position to play within it."
- "To have _dignity_ is to feel worthy. All children are worthy of respect, caring, love, thought, and courtesy."
- Children need an _opportunity_ to grow and develop, which means that "young people must be able to explore and express their capabilities without undue external barriers. Children must have access to quality education, recreation and leisure, all at an appropriate developmental level.[14]" **5**

I might also add that spiritual and moral nurturing would be one of my top reasons for giving children a good start in life. In fact, I would probably list it as number one.

"The point is that children's needs are fairly basic and relatively easy to identify and categorize. The tough task is ensuring that children get the basics." **6**

This brings us to the permanent temporary care children - those children who are consistently placed in foster home after foster home - never developing any permanence in childhood. A very critical question could be asked here, "Might a child that would fall under this permanent temporary category be better helped by being exposed to a children's home where he/she would be exposed to the things that would create <u>connectedness, continuity, dignity, opportunity, and spiritual nurturing?</u>

The reputation that most orphanages received in the first fifty years of the twentieth century (1900-1950) is generally understood to be very distorted. There were some bad orphanages or children's homes during this time, but it is also understood that a great number of these institutions were very well run and provided excellent care for many boys and girls.

It is also generally accepted that these institutions have received a "bad rap" and, in quite a number of cases, the things that were alleged to have happened did not happen. The image and bad reputation has, however, remained.

"As a group, the alumni (orphanages) *have outpaced their counterparts in the general population by significant margins on practically all measures, not the least of which are education, income, and attitude toward life. The survey respondents seem to be saying that they got from their orphanage experience the required, <u>"connectedness, continuity, dignity</u> and <u>opportunity</u>" that constituted a "good start" and served them well later in life.*[18]*"* [7]

"The survey details are available in a scholarly journal. I mention here, though, that the orphanage alumni who are now forty-eight and older have a 17 percent higher high school graduation rate than their counterparts in the general population and a 39 percent higher college graduation rate. They also have significantly more professional master's degrees and more doctorates. Social commentators often fret

that the cycles of poverty, abuse, and neglect cannot be broken, but the median household incomes of the orphanage alumni were one-tenth to three-fifth's higher (depending on age group) than the medians for their counterparts in the general population. Moreover, the orphans' rate of unemployment, poverty, incarceration, and dependence on public assistance were minor fractions of the rates for other white Americans." [8]

These statistics say to us that long-term permanent care has outstanding advantages. Some of which are: **(1) a sense of security and belonging; (2) educational opportunity; (3) a positive work ethic; (5) spiritual and moral nurturing; (5) the building of lifelong relationships; and (6) a sense of belonging.**

Some so-called "experts" seem to be convinced that any family care (no matter what type it is) is better than the best institutional care. Research and surveys do not bear out this premise. It is always sad when parent and custodial rights are terminated; but to say that any family care is better than institutional care is just simply not true.

Money is the great common denominator when decisions regarding foster homes vs. orphanage care are determined. Most states pay an average of four to six hundred dollars per month per child to foster care parents. The average institutional (orphanage) care cost annually is close to $25,000.00 to $30,000.00. Unfortunately, you can see that money is the big denominator regarding child-care decision making when it comes to foster care vs. children's home care.

Some major reasons that institutional costs have risen so quickly revolve around not only the increased quality of care, but increased number and quality of outstanding and dedicated staff. Institutionalized children are consistently being cared for in a more professional manner in all areas of their lives: <u>physically, morally, emotionally, spiritually, socially, and recreationally</u>.

When I was at Connie Maxwell all of these things were given to me in abundance. There is no way I will ever be able to say "thank you" for all I was given at Connie Maxwell. I did not have a very high awareness level of what was being done for me at that time, but I do now. I also realize how fortunate I was to have been given all the opportunities that I was given. Even though I wanted to be with my own family, I was taken out of a situation that took me off the streets of Greenville, SC and put me in a caring, Christian environment that was directly responsible for me being the success I am now in the year 2000.

When I was at Connie Maxwell, the average number of children in each home was somewhere between twenty to twenty-five with eight to ten children to a room. Each home had only a matron or cottage mother.

In the year 2000, the average number is eight – two to a room. The homes are smaller now and most homes have a mother and a father (a married couple.)

We went off campus to sporting events, to go to school, and on Saturday afternoon we were permitted to go to town and to a movie. Most all of the children in the year 2000 are involved in every aspect of school activities such as annual staff, debating club, all sports, etc. This practice is extremely positive in turning good children into good adults, ready for the problems of the real world.

There was not a great deal of counseling or therapy when I was on campus. The orphanage of today is involved in extensive group and personal therapy and counseling. Several years ago Connie Maxwell built an outdoor adventure ropes training course where students are taught to work together as a team and solve problems together. This provides therapy in a different way than personal counseling. Most orphanages are doing the same things. Their philosophy tends to be <u>"we want this child to be well adjusted when he/she leaves our care so that he/she can handle the problems/situations they will encounter as adults."</u>

The basic philosophy of Connie Maxwell has always been to pull out all the stops regarding keeping the family as a workable, loving, mature unit together.

The average length of time that a child will stay at Connie Maxwell in 2000 is thirty to thirty-six months. I personally stayed seven years. There are always a number of students who will stay until they finish high school. Some children know that the worst place they could be is the very dysfunctional home situation from which they came. They choose to stay at Connie Maxwell. They seem to know they are better off at an institution. Most children have an almost uncanny way of knowing when they are loved and accepted and when they are not and can make some of those critical family decisions as maturely as adults.

"We must find a way to ensure that private charities, religious organizations, and civic groups can develop creative alternative institutional-care opportunities that meet the local needs of identified populations of children. To clear the way for development of care options, two changes are necessary:

• Private homes and their supporting religious, civic, and charitable organizations must be given greater freedom to devise methods of care that are more cost effective.

• More children must enter permanent institutional care before they have been repeatedly abused, have experienced prolonged stays in the foster-care system, and have become troubled by the lack of permanence in their lives. [30] " **9**

In closing this chapter, I would like to share with you some ideas that I gleaned from a self-help book entitled, "*Parent and Child*" by Heim Genett.

These things will help me grow and become successful.

    1. **Give your critic a face and a name.**
        If you have someone in your past that was abusive and/or mean to you, identify the person or persons. Get yourself a legal pad and write out the actual name or names of people who were not pleasant or nice to you and who created negative feelings toward the world and your situation.

    2. **Identify who programmed you.**

Let God be your guide. Identify who or what created the attitude you now hold in your heart and mind. Ask yourself several questions:

        a.   Who or what programmed me?
                  Was I aware of being programmed?
        b.   Do I know why and how I was programmed?
        c.   Am I happy with my program?
        d.   If I'm not happy, why?
        e.   Would I like to change my program?
        f.   In what way(s) would I change it?

3. **Notice when you critic comes alive**.

For several years after I left Connie Maxwell, I had a tendency to get angry easily. That personal flaw caused me to lose some friends and to have some strained relationships. I didn't realize how angry I was at my father for his drinking and lax moral problems.   I would not confront him. My anger came out every time I was around him or had anything to do with him. As I gained new insights, I was able to raise my self-awareness level and manage my anger.

If you pay special attention to when these feelings arise and what causes them, then you can either avoid those situations or learn to deal with them appropriately.

4. **Know when to press the "DELETE" button**.

Learn to identify when these <u>feelings</u> and emotions are in charge of you. Then you <u>can press the delete button on the recorder inside your head.</u> You cannot completely get rid of them but you can make them work for you. George Compton, my coach at Connie Maxwell during baseball season, gave me some excellent advice. I was playing third base and I kept letting the ball go through my legs. I asked Coach Compton what I could do and he said, "You are letting the ball play you; you play the ball." I have never forgotten that. What he was really saying to me was, "You play life, don't let life play you."

My cottage mother at Eastern Star my first three years at Connie Maxwell was Mrs. Windham. We got along like oil and water – nothing about our personalities ever meshed. I think both of us were pretty unhappy. I know that I was. I graduated from Connie Maxwell in 1954 and Mrs. Windham died in 1955. Even though we didn't get along very well, I always felt I needed to talk with her and somehow make right our relationship. So, in 1985, I did a little detective work and found out through the Bureau of Vital Statistics that she was buried at a little cemetery in Branchville, SC.

I made up my mind to go to Branchville where she was buried and "talk to her." I followed through with my commitment to myself and we had a really good talk for about an hour. I asked her to forgive me and I told her that I forgave her. It meant nothing to anyone except me. I realized I needed to press the "delete" button, once and for all.

Another way to press the "delete" button is to write a letter to the offending party, detailing everything you feel that you need to get off your chest. Keep the letter handy for a few weeks – read it one last time and tear it up. It has served its purpose. Then get on with your life.

5. **Everything that ever happens to you is a teacher.**

When we keep an accounting of who "ticks us off" and who doesn't, we miss the point of the real lesson that comes out of the experience. A friend of mine taught me a very valuable lesson when he invited me to develop an attitude of "THAT'S GOOD" and then start looking for the good in the situation. He became a millionaire at age 38.

I think there are times when an individual needs to "junk" a bad experience, a bad relationship, a bad decision, a bad marriage, even a bad childhood. Life goes on. We can grow and become bigger, better, stronger, and wiser if we can learn from the experience. We can touch the lives of other people who may need our help or encouragement in a similar experience. I hope you will consider the words of this little treatise:

JUNK IT

Junk something everyday.

Junk your worries, junk your fears, junk your anxieties, junk your little jealousies, junk your envies, and junk your hatreds – whatever interferes with your getting up and getting on in the world. Junk It!

Every night before you go to sleep, put in the junk heap all of your disappointments, your grudges, your desires for revenge, your malice. Junk every thing, which is, in any way, hindering you from being a strong, fine person and a success.

The great trouble with most of us is that we don't have a junk heap of this sort. We are afraid to scrap anything for fear we shall need it some day.

Consequently, we pull all our mental enemies, all our handicaps, all our discouragement, all our losses, all our misfortunes, all our troubles, all our worries, and all our trials along with us.

This huge load of rubbish saps more than fifty percent of our vitality and energy, so that we have only a relatively small amount of strength remaining with which to tackle the great achievements of going places and doing things in life.

We are weighted down with excess baggage. The beauty of our lives is befogged by the heaps of junk which clutter up our days. If there is something in your life that you do not need, which is weighing you down,

JUNK IT!
That's what trash piles are for!

--Author Unknown

"When my spirit grows faint within me, it is You who know my way." Psalm 142:3 NIV

AND REMEMBER,

**IF IT
IS TO BE,
IT IS
UP TO ME**

"O Lord, You are my God, I will exalt You, I will praise your name, for You have done wonderful things; Your counsels of old are faithfulness and truth."

Isaiah 25:1 NKJV

STAFF - WHAT PART DO THEY PLAY?

Chapter 6

"One hundred years from now it will not matter
what kind of car I drove, what kind of house I lived in,
how much money I had in my bank account,
nor what my clothes looked like.

But one hundred years from now the world may be a little
better because I was important in the life of a child.'

--Unknown

The possibility that I will ever be able to do justice to this
chapter really does not exist. The one critical element of the
mental health and development of self-esteem in a child rests
in the staff of any orphanage or children's home.

Dr. Jimmy McAdams made a tour of a number of Baptist
Children's Homes in several states in the spring of 1999. He
wrote about his experiences and what he discovered about how
other children's homes were being run and what their mission
involved. I dedicate this chapter to him and have received his
permission to use his dedication from the book titled, "Baptist
Children's Homes in America: A First Hand Look."

DEDICATION
"This work is affectionately dedicated to the hundreds of
direct-care staff who serve in residential child care programs
of Southern Baptists. The individuals who devote themselves
to the daily care of dependent children are simply special
people. Most often, they come to their roles with a deep sense

of calling, a summons that keeps them at their posts of duty long past the time when mere hirelings have fled. Their thrills come from witnessing children they have loved grow and improve. They invest ample amounts of patience and learn to celebrate minuscule progress. They understand, to a greater degree than any other group of people, the extremes of the emotional continuum. Their journals reveal an acquaintance with both joy and sorrow.

"For those who have endured, there is that unexplainable pleasure of seeing the fruits of their labors: Children who spend formative years under their tutelage come back to say thanks. Often these returnees share reports of strong families, stable jobs, completed degrees, and positions of leadership in their churches. More often than not, they credit the campus experiences with the good that has happened in their lives."

--Jimmy McAdams

The fact that he chose to dedicate the book to "staff" members helped me develop a deeper respect for Dr. McAdams. He recognizes the important role that staff members play in the lives of hurting and displaced children. I could not agree with him more. I sincerely hope this chapter will help you realize, as I have, that the most critical influence in the lives of hurting children is capable and serious staff personnel.

The writing of this book has created more uncanny coincidences that you can imagine. I have received many rewarding stories from countless numbers of people. These stories have touched my heart and have given me much material and many insights. I would like to share one of those stories with you (as given to me by Jerry Friedner, a Connie Maxwell alumnus.)

THE LITTLE TEDDY STODDARD STORY -- A story is told of an elementary teacher named Mrs. Thompson. As she stood in front of her fifth grade class on the very first day of school, she told the children a lie. Like most teachers, she looked at her students and said that she loved them all the same.

But that was impossible, because there in the front row, slumped in his seat was a little boy named Teddy Stoddard. Mrs. Thompson had watched Teddy the year before and noticed that he didn't play well with the other children, that his clothes were messy and that he constantly needed a bath. Teddy could be unpleasant. It got to the point where Mrs. Thompson would actually take delight in marking his papers with a broad red pen, making bold X's and then putting a big "F" at the top.

At the school where Mrs. Thompson taught, she was required to review each child's past records and she put Teddy's off until last. However, when she reviewed his file, she was in for a surprise.

Teddy's first grade teacher wrote, "Teddy is a bright child with a ready laugh. He does his work neatly and has good manners...he is a joy to be around."

His second grade teacher wrote, "Teddy is an excellent student, well liked by his classmates; but he is troubled because his mother has a terminal illness and life at home must be a struggle."

His third grade teacher wrote, "His mother's death has been hard on him. He tries to do his best, but his father doesn't show much interest in his home life and this will soon affect him if some steps aren't taken."

Teddy's fourth grade teacher wrote, "Teddy is withdrawn and doesn't show much interest in school. He doesn't have many friends and he sometimes sleeps in class."

By now, Mrs. Thompson realized the problem and was ashamed of her self. She felt even worse when her students brought her Christmas presents which were wrapped in beautiful ribbons and bright paper - all except for Teddy's. His present was clumsily wrapped in the heavy, brown paper that he got from a grocery bag.

Mrs. Thompson took pains to open it in the middle of the other presents. Some of the children started to laugh when she found a rhinestone bracelet with some the stones missing, and a bottle that was one quarter full of perfume. But she stifled the children's laughter when she exclaimed how pretty the bracelet was, putting it on, and dabbing some of the perfume on her wrist. Teddy Stoddard stayed after school that day just long enough to say, "Mrs. Thompson, today you smelled just like my Mom used to."

After the children left she cried for at least an hour. On that very day, she quit teaching reading, and writing, and arithmetic. Instead, she began to teach children.

Mrs. Thompson paid particular attention to Teddy. As she worked with him, his mind seemed to come alive. The more she encouraged him, the faster he responded. By the end of the year, Teddy had become one of the smartest children in the class and, despite her lie that she would love all the children the same, Teddy became one of her "teacher's pets."

A year later, she found a note under her door, from Teddy, telling her that she was still the best teacher he ever had in his whole life.

Six years went by before she got another note from Teddy. He then wrote that he had finished high school, third in his class, and she was still the best teacher he ever had in this whole life.

Four years later, she got another letter saying that while things had been tough at times, he'd stayed in school, stuck with it, and would soon graduate from college with the highest of honors. He assured Mrs. Thompson that she was still the best and favorite teacher he ever had in his whole life.

Then four more years passed and yet another letter came. This time he explained that after he got his bachelor's degree, he decided to go a little further. The letter explained that she was still the best and favorite teacher he ever had. But now his name was a little longer - the letter was signed, Theodore F. Stoddard, M.D.

The story doesn't end there. There was yet another letter that spring. Teddy said he'd met this girl and was going to be married. He explained that his father had died a couple of years ago and he was wondering if Mrs. Thompson might agree to sit in the place at the wedding that was usually reserved for the mother of the groom.

Of course, Mrs. Thompson did. And guess what? She wore that bracelet, the one with several rhinestones missing. And she made sure she was wearing the perfume that Teddy remembered his mother wearing on their last Christmas together. They hugged each other, and Dr. Stoddard whispered in Mrs. Thompson's ear, "Thank you, Mrs. Thompson for believing in me. Thank you so much for making me feel important and showing me that I could make a difference."

Mrs. Thompson, with tears in her eyes, whispered back. She said, "Teddy, you have it all wrong. You were the one who taught me that I could make a difference. I didn't know how to teach until I met you."

I thought you would also like to know that Jerry Friedner was the winner of a contest that John Sheriff (alumni president) had several years ago to come up with a theme for our alumni reunions. The theme that was chosen was the one Jerry had submitted: "Connie Maxwell Made A Difference."

There were several people at Connie Maxwell that made a big difference in my life. One of those was Mr. M. J. "Dick" Rhodes who was the farm manager when I came to Connie Maxwell and for quite a few years after I left. He trusted me, he believed in me, he encouraged me, and he gave me a tremendous amount of responsibility.

I wanted to earn extra money every chance I could, so I would work on Saturday afternoon, especially in the spring and fall. Some of the other boys and girls went to town to the movies on Saturday afternoon, but I got more satisfaction out of working even though it was only for thirty-five cents an hour. I did mostly farm work. I liked to plow and I liked to drive the big "M" farm tractor. If I started on Saturday morning (when all of us had to work anyway for nothing) I could usually go home for lunch and then return and continue plowing until six or seven at night. I could count exactly how much I was going to make that afternoon and dream about what I would buy. I always liked to dress very nicely and would spend some of "my" money to buy clothes. This is not to imply that I wasn't well clothed while I was at Connie Maxwell, because I was.

All of us had what we called "box" parents. Box parents were a church or a group of parents that would take us for a weekend to the city where they lived and buy us one hundred fifty to two hundred dollars worth of clothes that would last us for six months or so. This would usually happen about twice a year, in early spring and late fall. None of us ever lacked for clothes or food, but it was always nice to know that we could buy some things simply because we wanted them.

There were a number of times that Mr. Rhodes didn't have a lot of extra work for me to do. So, he would be creative and find something for me. That something might be two of us working together on a crosscut saw. We had to cut a cord of wood. We were basically paid on production. If we didn't produce, we didn't get paid. If we did produce, we got paid accordingly. I always made it a point to choose someone who would be opposite of me on the cross-cut saw that wasn't lazy and would do his share of the pulling. You never push a cross-cut saw, so I wanted to make sure I had a good "puller" so we could both cut more wood and earn more money. It was a lesson that Mr. Rhodes knew would stay with us for life, and it has.

I have been appalled at my ignorance in not learning and applying some of those lessons he taught me until many years after I left Connie Maxwell. I'm sure I didn't realize some very important lessons he was trying to teach me at the time; but I have come to the conclusion that some lessons in life don't come until years after they have been taught. I will always be grateful for Mr. M. J. "Dick" Rhodes.

I am also sure I am not the only one that he "taught." Mr. Rhodes must have helped literally hundreds of young boys who needed encouragement and a strong hand to point them in the right direction.

Another staff member that was very important in my life at Connie Maxwell was the vegetable farm manager, Mr. Bill Clyburn – affectionately known to us as "Mr. C." He was a very gentle but firm man. The minute you met him you knew he was a man's man. He could be soft and gentle and he could be firm and resolute. You knew the very second you met him that you were someone special. He was always willing to listen to you and offer the kind of soft advice that he knew you needed but probably didn't want to hear.

He was a very mannerly and courteous man. If I live to be two hundred years old, I will never forget one thing he said to me (that didn't register until much later in my life). We were talking one day about being nice to people; and he said, "<u>Gene, manners and courtesy will take you further in life than money, wealth or fame</u>." I cannot tell you how many times in my life that statement has come true for me. It was evident that he had a class and style about him that set him apart. I cannot think of a time when he ever scolded or shouted at me. His softness and resoluteness was a combination that I personally have tried to copy. He talked to us and led us by example – I will never forget the life he led and the examples he set. I feel about "Mr. C" the same way that I feel about Mr. Rhodes. I'm sure there are literally hundreds of boys that he influenced that are much better today than they would have been had it not been for "Mr. C."

The best thing that I could do for both of these men, as well as so many other staff members, who touched my life in a positive way, is to dedicate this little short "composition" to them.

What is Class

Class never runs scared. It is sure-footed and confident in the knowledge that you can meet life head on and handle whatever comes along.

Jacob had it. Esau did not. Symbolically, we can look to Jacob's wrestling match with the angel. Those who have class have wrestled with their own personal "angel" and won a victory that marks them thereafter.

Class never makes excuses. It takes its lumps and learns from past mistakes.

Class is considerate of others. It knows that good manners are nothing more than a series of petty sacrifices.

Class bespeaks an aristocracy that has nothing to do with ancestors or money. The most affluent

Blue-blood can be totally without class while the descendant of a Welsh miner may ooze class from every pore.

Class never tries to build itself up by tearing others down. Class is already up and needs not strive to look better by making others look worse.

Class can "walk with kings and keep its virtue; talk with crowds and keep the common touch." Everyone is comfortable with the person who has class because he is comfortable with himself.

If you have class, you don't need much of anything else. If you don't have it, no matter what else you have, it doesn't make much difference.

--Author Unknown

I am a great believer in stories and parables – one of the major teaching methods that Jesus used to teach the multitudes as well as his disciples. This is another one of those stories that was shared with me after I started writing this book. I have felt God's hand literally hundreds of times since I realized the Connie Maxwell story must be told by someone who had "been there and done that." It came from my son, Mark.

T. J. Wrote on the Wall

A weary mother returned from the store,
Lugging groceries through the kitchen door.
Awaiting her arrival was her 8-year-old son,
Anxious to relate what his younger brother had done.

"While I was out playing and Dad was on a call,
T.J. took his crayons and wrote on the wall!
It's on the new paper you just hung in the den.
I told him you'd be mad at having to do it again."

She let out a moan and furrowed her brow.
"Where is your little brother right now?"
She emptied her arms and with a purposeful stride,
She marched to this closet where he had gone to hide.

She called his full name as she entered his room.
He trembled with fear-he knew that meant doom.
For the next ten minutes, she ranted and raved
About the expensive wallpaper and how she had saved.

Lamenting all the work it would take to repair,
She condemned his actions and total lack of care.
The more she scolded, the madder she got,
Then stomped from his room, totally distraught!

She headed for the den to confirm her fears.
When she saw the wall, her eyes flooded with tears.
The message she read pierced her soul with a dart.
It said, "I love Mommy" and was surrounded by a heart.

Well, the wallpaper remained, just as she found it,
With an empty picture frame hung to surround it.
A reminder to her, and indeed to all,
Take time to read the handwriting on the wall.

--Author unknown

I have become keenly aware in the last few years how important it is to let people know how much you appreciate them when they have filled a very special void in your life. Psychologists could call that "network building," but I call it just plain old appreciation. I have been a little mad at myself that I didn't do more "appreciating" to those who had my best interest at heart. In the year 2000 we call those individuals "mentors," but the word doesn't seem to be adequate enough. I am not sure what that word would be but I am sure that I have had a number of people in my life, especially at Connie Maxwell, that always seemed to be there for me when I needed them.

I wish I could name all the "mentors" I have had but that's impossible. However, I can name a few. Dr. Sam Smith would certainly top the list as I have dedicated this book to him. Others include: Dr. Jimmy McAdams, Mr. M. J. Rhodes, Mr. William B. Clyburn ("Mr. C"), Mary Deloache who was my social worker at Connie Maxwell, Ben and Polly Davis, Iris Bullard, John Sheriff, Eric Taylor, Randy McManus, Mrs. Maude Gosnell, Mrs. Estell Hawkins, Mrs. Grace Holtzclaw (our campus nurse in the forties, fifties and sixties), Scott James, Mack Baltzegar, Harold Driggers, Dean Mahaffey, John Sheriff and many, many more that are too numerous to mention.

This part of chapter six has been reserved for my very special mentor, Dr. Sam Smith. "Dr. Sam" as we affectionately called him, came to Connie Maxwell as a very young boy at nine years of age. He had not been attending school and was far behind the other children. To make a very long story short, Dr. Smith did catch up in school. He finished high school and went to Furman University. After he earned his degree, he went to work at Connie Maxwell under the helpful wing of Dr. Atha

Jamison. Dr. Jamison was the superintendent at Connie Maxwell for forty-six years. When Dr. Jamison died, Dr. Smith was appointed as his successor and also, served for forty-six years. During that time a number of changes took place at Connie Maxwell, which continued to make it a place of refuge and safety for hurting, and displaced children.

In 1946, under Dr. Smith's tenure, the name was changed from Connie Maxwell Orphanage to Connie Maxwell Children's Home. An operational budget for the home was approved for the first time in its history. It was also learned at that time that 84.5% of the 1,242 Baptist Churches in the state contributed something to Connie Maxwell. The population of Connie Maxwell was beginning to go down because of the establishment of many more orphanages and children's homes in the state. Population on campus in 1956 was two hundred, eighty-six children. In 1966, the Community based home was established. In 1977, the population was at one hundred, twenty-five children.

Dr. Smith was recognized, not only in South Carolina but all over the nation, as an agent for change in the ministering of services for hurting children. Dr. Smith's attitude was probably like a little story I recently found about a father and his boys playing in the yard. It goes something like this:

> My Father used to play with my brother and me in the yard. Mother would come out and say, "You're tearing up the grass." "We're not raising grass," my dad would reply, "we're raising *boys.*"

A very dear Connie Maxwell sister, Leslie Taylor, in an article published in the *USA Today Newspaper* dated March 22, 2000 says, "When (Dr. Sam) spoke to you his voice had a resonance." Taylor recalls "You found yourself just wanting to hear everything he had to say. And he said it with such kindness. And he spoke so respectfully, you knew he cared."

I was very fortunate to be asked to speak at a special ceremony for "Dr. Sam" on August 27, 1995. He was awarded the Order of the Palmetto – one of the most coveted awards given by the governor of the state of South Carolina to only a handful of its most valued citizens. That event is one of the highlights of my life – I shall never forget it.

I could go on for hours about how influential this man has been in my life as well as the lives of literally hundreds of other alumni of Connie Maxwell Children's Home.

I was saddened to hear of his continued failing health and that, eventually, he had to be placed in the Martha Franks Nursing Home in Laurens, SC.

Dean Mahaffey, who was serving as a Connie Maxwell trustee, and I, who was also a trustee at the time, had our regular quarterly trustee's meeting in Greenwood the first Thursday in November 1997. She was driving back to Spartanburg and I was driving back to Greenville. We decided that we would like to go by Laurens and see "Dr. Sam." Some staff members had told us he was having some good days and some bad days. Some days he had an excellent memory and some days he was very addled and "out of it." We had no idea how we would find him that Thursday afternoon, but both of us knew we wanted to go. He was so dear to us. We got to the nursing home and found him in excellent condition in mind and body. He was the soft, humble, quiet, unassuming "Dr. Sam" that we knew and loved. We both kneeled beside him in that waiting room where there were fifteen or twenty other people and talked to him for four or five minutes. I will never forget what he said to Dean and me. We both assumed that he was referring to the fact that we were both trustees at the time. He said, "I hear you are both doing an excellent job." I don't remember to this day what we said back to him, but I looked at Dean and she looked back at me, and we both were on the verge of tears. Somehow we didn't cry and somehow we carried on while we were in his presence. The time passed quickly and we left. Neither one of us could say a word. We just held hands and tried to be brave and composed as we walked down the hall and back to our autos. We cried all the way back to our cars. Dean finally said, "I'm glad we came, this may be the last time we will ever see him alive." He passed away only six weeks later. Neither of us has ever regretted that visit to this day and I'm sure we never will.

I'm sure "Dr. Sam" would be pleased with this poem I ran across recently in one of the many publications that I read.

MY INFLUENCE

My life shall touch a dozen lives
Before this day is done,
Leave countless marks of good or ill,
Ere sets the evening sun.
This, the wish I always wish,
The prayer I always pray:
Lord, may my life help other lives
It touches by the way.

I was at the Connie Maxwell offices several months ago and went by to see Joann Dodgens. Joann had worked with "Dr. Sam" for, as she says, "<u>23 years, 2 months, and 21 days</u>." She wrote about Dr. Sam and, with her permission, I share it with you.

THE GREATEST MAN I EVER KNEW

"The greatest man I ever knew was Dr. Sam M. Smith, whom I met 23 years, 2 months and 21 days ago - the day I came to work at Connie Maxwell Children's Home - such a long and yet such a short time ago. He was a quiet gentleman, with a heart as big as the sky, and it breaks my heart in two—to have to say goodbye.

No longer will I see him at my office door, smiling like he always did, and he would ask, "Mrs. Dodgens, do you have a minute, I need your help once more?"

It might be a letter to a senator or a stranger who took him home one night or to one of his Connie Maxwell kids who had honored him – and I would type his letter right.

He never told you how to live—you saw it in him every day. To be like him, I wish I could—in every single way.

The greatest man I ever knew is before us here today. The love and respect I have for him, I know each of you share it, too. You could not know this man and not feel how great he was. The tears we shed today are for his family, too, for they have lost the greatest man I ever knew.

On December 18, 1997, at the age of 92, our God called him home to heaven, as I knew someday soon – he would. Heaven will be a better place with him up there, and don't you know how great it will be for all his Connie Maxwell kids to see him there! The greatest man I ever knew!"

--Joann Dodgens

I cannot say enough or write enough about "Connie Maxwell staff members" and the part they have played in the lives of hurting children. Cottage mothers (cottage parents as they are now called) are at the very top of my list. They see the children every day. They see them well and sick, good and bad, moody and in good spirits, hurting when no family or friends come to see them, or when (as happened just recently) graduation time comes and not one single member of their family shows up. The cottage parents hurt and agonize over the hurts of "<u>their children</u>."

My personal attachment to Mrs. Maude ("Hon") Gosnell still warms my heart to his day. She was soft, quiet, and loving but you knew when she said <u>NO</u>, it meant <u>NO</u>. I will take her wonderful memory with me always.

<u>I now close this chapter feeling that I will never be able to adequately say or write about how important the Connie Maxwell staff members are in the life of a hurting child.</u> This little short story may come close.

I MADE YOU

"On the street I saw a small girl, cold and shivering in a thin dress, with little hope of a decent meal. I became angry and said to God, "Why did you permit this? Why don't you

115

do some thing about it?"

For a while God said nothing. That night, quite suddenly, He replied, "I certainly did do something about it -- I made you.""

--Author Unknown

I would like to say to every staff member at Connie Maxwell something very, very, very personal. It is these four things:

1. I sincerely believe you have been called to a ministry as surely as a minister in the pulpit has.

2. I sincerely believe that God will guard you and give you the strength you need to do the ministry to which you have been called.

3. I sincerely believe there will be times when you will question your commitment and resolve – this is normal – those are the times when you are growing – God is still so close to you that you can feel his breath.

4. I sincerely believe there will be times when you, your commitment and your help will go unappreciated. Rest assured that the real lessons that children are learning while under your care, sometimes go years before they realize how much you did for them; how much you cared for them; and how much you worried about their welfare. Believe me, I know---I'm one of them.

-----Gene Bishop

"Religion that God our Father accepts as pure and faultless is this: to look after orphans and widows in their distress and to keep oneself from being polluted by the world." James 1:27 NIV

AND REMEMBER,

IT IF
IS TO BE,
IT IS
UP TO ME

"But the fruit of the Spirit is love, joy, peace, long-suffering, kindness, goodness, faithfulness..."

Galatians 5:22 NKJV

WHAT HAPPENED TO THE DAVIS FAMILY?

Chapter 7

I've learned that if you stay focused on yourself, you are guaranteed to be miserable.

What were some of the circumstances that brought you to Connie Maxwell?

My sisters, Nellie and Louise, and I were admitted to Connie Maxwell on November 4, 1930. The reason for this was a tragic event that took place on the property of The Charleston & Western Carolina Railroad on August 1, 1929, in Spartanburg, SC.

A mentally disturbed man wielding a hatchet struck five railroad employees. One was injured severely, but survived. Four were killed almost instantly. My father was one of the four killed.

Also, a factor that caused us to go to Connie Maxwell was failure on the part of the bank that held our family savings. Practically all our money went down the tube. The very same thing happened to many families during the peak years of the big depression of the twenties and thirties.

The trip to Connie Maxwell to be admitted was on November 4, 1930. It all started with the thought that the three of us kids were going for a ride in the country. There was a Red Cross lady, or it could have been a social worker from Connie Maxwell, who was to pick us up for this ride in the country. It was a long ride through out the morning and well into the latter part of the afternoon. Our mother went with us but my two younger sisters did not go. My mother took care of the youngest two by operating a boarding house – meals and lodging for Southern Railroad Employees in Spartanburg, SC.

The trip "through the country" ended on the campus of Connie Maxwell. The matron of the cottage met the Red Cross woman and my mother at the car where we stopped. I learned later this woman was Mrs. Vera Smith. All three women entered the cottage. We kids were attracted to the playground swings and seesaw. Nellie and I were on a seesaw – I bumped her off -- she cried and held her breath. This disturbed me and I ran inside the cottage looking for my mother. I learned of some bad news. My mother and the Red Cross woman had left. Of course, this was disturbing to all of us kids and we didn't get over it right away.

I found out later that it was an accepted practice at that time to leave children without having a hassle. Well, I don't know of a better way, but I still think of it in a negative way.

What are some negative experiences that happened at Connie Maxwell while you were there?

This experience was a bad one, but I brought it on myself. I broke one of the rules and I paid the price. During the summer months the swimming pool was a wonderful attraction for us children. The boys had separate days for swimming than the girls had. The girls used the pool on Mondays and Fridays – the boys on Tuesdays and Saturdays. This schedule did not change in my eleven years at Connie Maxwell.

Late in the afternoon on one of the girls' days, I found myself in the pool enjoying swimming. The girls had left for the day. I had it all to myself. In less than ten minutes a staff member appeared in the pool area. He didn't say a word – just looked me over and disappeared. Shortly after this happened, I lost interest in the swimming and returned to my cottage. My matron told me to report to one of the staff members at the office. I knew I was in trouble. This man that saw me in the pool had a history of reporting us kids for minor infractions of the rules.

The staff member that I reported to at the office told me to obtain a sling blade and rake and spend the next three days cleaning out poison oak from the pool area. This I did for only two days. My matron went to bat for me at the end of the second day. She told the staff member that assigned me this punishment that I was covered with poison oak – blisters from head to toe – and I was. My matron did not allow any further working in the pool area. My matron doctored me for over a week before I got over this mess. What a price I paid for a few minutes of pleasure. The moral of this story – "If you dance you must pay the fiddler."

What are some positive experiences that you had at Connie Maxwell?

My sister, Nellie, after she had run away, was transferred to Greenwood Cottage. This was a positive experience for both of us. I knew she would love Miss Josie and she did.

Working at the storeroom was quiet an experience. There were many folks that I saw regularly. There was a time when I knew practically everyone on campus, boys and girls.

Dr. Jamison was an inspiration to me. I saw him frequently at the office. He was the neatest dressed person I've ever known. He was that way every day.

Name 2 or 3 staff members that had a very special impact on shaping your live at Connie Maxwell?

The following staff members I hold in my highest esteem:
Dr. A. T. Jamison, Superintendent
Miss Josie Hardin, Matron, Greenwood Cottage
Miss Susie Newbold, Supervisor, Store Room
Mr. M. J. Rhodes, Supervisor, Dairy

I trusted then as righteous people and they expected the same of me.

Explain some things that happened to you that brought you success because of what you learned or experienced at Connie Maxwell.

While at Connie Maxwell I was assigned several jobs. I did them well because I knew it was expected of me. I developed an attitude that my supervisors were interested in me and I didn't care to let them down. I never got chewed out for doing a lousy job or being tardy. I left Connie Maxwell with the feeling that I was a dependable and responsible person. Doing a day's work was nothing new to me. These are some of the things that helped me get a good job and keep it.

How was your cottage mother an influence (negative or positive) on you?

As I remember, I was at Greenwood Cottage approximately seven years and Miss Josie Hardin was my matron.

I was transferred from Terrell Smith Home to Greenwood Cottage. I ran away twice while at Terrill Smith Home. I don't know if that was the reason for the transfer or not but must say somebody was on my side. I did not enjoy Terrill Smith Home. I was at this place for four years.

I learned to love Miss Josie immediately. She came to Connie Maxwell as a schoolteacher. There was a need for a matron and Miss Josie asked for the assignment and was accepted.

Miss Josie was "the world's greatest cook." She was my salvation. She knew how to solve algebra and geometry problems, and she was good at English as well. I was not the only one she helped – it seemed to be an everyday occurrence. She stayed up late and was always willing to stay as long as necessary for us to understand the problems.

I will never forget this experience. Just a day or two before Christmas there was a little boy at Greenwood Cottage that hadn't received anything for Christmas – one present. Miss Josie went to town and bought him presents with her own money. She would never let a little boy go through an experience of not having presents when everyone else had them.

Another experience I won't forget. I had been in service, World War II for three years. When I was discharged, I went over to Chester to see Miss Josie – she had retired. I stopped at a drug store to call because I didn't want to surprise her. I really wanted to give her a few minutes to pretty up. Most women fix their hair and powder their face. I dialed her number and when she answered I asked her if she knew who was calling. She said, without hesitating, "It's Frank Davis."

Her mind and eyesight was keen as a young person and she was in her eighties. If there is anybody I loved, it was Miss Josie Hardin. I have a picture of her and one of Greenwood Cottage in my den. Hardly a day will pass that I don't look at both.

Did you play any sports at Connie Maxwell? What were they and did they influence you at Connie Maxwell and/or after you left?

Yes, I played football, baseball and some basketball.

Dr. Smith was the athletic director while I was at Connie Maxwell. Of course he was concerned about winning games, but obeying the rules of the game was just as important.

He expected you to never argue with the umpire's decision; never spike a player; never throw a bat; obey the rules; and become a good sport. You either obeyed the rules or you didn't play on Dr. Smith's team.

Also, part of the process of being a good ball player was that you must practice regularly. All these rules certainly apply to many things in life other than sports. For instance, practice – try sawing a straight line without instruction or practice. Arguing can certainly get you in lots of trouble. Being a good sport does have merit.

What school activities in Greenwood were you involved in?

In my ninth year I was a school boy patrolman at Greenwood High School. I directed traffic so students could cross safely on the north end of the street in front of the high school.

During the spring of that school year, there was a National Convention in Washington, DC for Schoolboy Patrolmen. As I recall, there were three of us boys from Connie Maxwell that were chosen. It was a four-day event. Two days in Washington and two days for travel.

Did you work on the farm, sewing room, print office, lunchroom, etc. and what are your thoughts on campus work – good or bad?

My work assignments were store room, office, and church. My main assignment was the storeroom. There was activity 5-1/2 days of the week at the storeroom. At church and at the office, I was responsible for janitorial services. At church it was only on Sunday and in the office it was five days per week.

Campus work was good for us. It helped us become responsible people who could be depended upon. When I left Connie Maxwell I was so accustomed to work that it was not a shock to my system.

Were you active in church activities? What did you do -- choir, usher, teach Sunday school?

When I was at Connie Maxwell each child was required to attend church services. When you came of age, you attended Sunday school and BYPU.

Staff members taught Sunday school and BYPU.

What were some things you did in your free time on campus – go to town, go to the movies, work, play, etc.?

I made model airplanes, raised pigeons, set rabbit boxes, sold candy around the campus, and played sports.

Model airplane building was my favorite past time, then and now. I have several radio controlled airplanes in my garage.

While at Connie Maxwell I had a six-foot model with a two-cycle engine. It was flown from the ball field after a ball game. The plane took off and drifted toward the city. There was a crowd of kids running down Maxwell Avenue trying to keep up with the direction it was going. I was in the crowd. I was so afraid of losing my airplane. I had sold candy nearly two years to buy the airplane and its engine.

The airplane finally gave out of gas and came down in the city. It hit the Oregon Hotel and then planked down the street near the post office. Very little damage occurred and I was able to repair it.

How are the things you learned at Connie Maxwell still shaping your life today?

There are many. I will mention only a few. I practice good health rules. I do not waste things. I am not afraid to do a day's work. I keep my house in order. I know how to make and keep friends and get along well with people.

Did you go to college when you left Connie Maxwell? Did Connie Maxwell help you financially?

No, I did not go to college. I pursued a technical career in aviation. I attended The Palmetto School of Aeronautics in Columbia, SC. I have an engine and aircraft license - a requirement if you work on airplanes.

I was in the Air Force during World War II. I was an electrical instructor – DC power systems on the B-29 airplanes.

I have worked on airplanes most of my working life. I retired from Delta Airlines in 1984 with thirty-four plus years of service. I was a mechanic, an engine inspector, and, for my last 13 years, I was the power plant foreman.

What advice would you have for children that are at Connie Maxwell now?

When you leave Connie Maxwell and select a career, within a reasonable length of time, you will be expected to develop good work skills. Even if you are highly productive, prompt, and a dependable skilled individual worker, there are several character traits that can easily disqualify you from advancement to positions of higher authority.

> Frequent criticizing.
> Frequent complaining.
> Frequent engaging in controversial issues.

Frequently engaging in anyone of the three can hurt you, just don't do it – rise above it.

Did you have any brothers or sisters at Connie Maxwell? Tell a little about them.

Yes, I had two sisters. The day I arrived I was eight years old, Nellie was six years old and Louise was ten years old. Nellie and I graduated the same year, 1941. Nellie and Louise both lived at Eason Home and their matron was Miss Hooten. Miss Annie Wells, the music teacher, lived there, also.

Nellie while living at Eason Home, under the supervision of a different matron, ran away, caught the bus and left town. She was in the tenth grade of high school when this happened.

When she arrived at my mother's boarding house in Spartanburg, SC she was very upset over a run-in she had with the new matron. My mother had a long talk with Dr. Jamison regarding the problem. He requested that Nellie be sent back. Nellie had only one day at home with our mother on this excursion.

A short time after Nellie returned, Dr. Jamison transferred her to Greenwood Cottage where I lived. It was wonderful having Nellie as our cook and seamstress.

What adjustments have you made (if any) when asked, "Where were you raised?"

I do not have a problem telling anyone that I was raised at Connie Maxwell Children's Home. The institution was called an orphanage during my years there, but I now prefer calling it "Children's Home." Neither do I use the word orphan as unfortunate. I was an orphan but not unfortunate.

Do you have a problem with your answers being used in a book centered on the life at Connie Maxwell?

I have no problems with any of my answers being used in a book. Gene, I fully endorse this project. I think it is a gesture of love to Connie Maxwell and Dr. Smith.

----Frank Davis

"He who is kind to the poor lends to the Lord, and He will reward him for what he has done."
Proverbs 19:17 NIV

Author's commentary: Frank Davis, like so many other Connie Maxwell alumni, is an outstanding example of how a child can grow to adulthood with the help of staff members that have the patience of Job. Every time I see Frank at our alumni reunions, we talk for hours. His attitude is always positive and helpful and it shows in his eyes and in his words. I am fortunate to call him my friend.

AND REMEMBER,

IF IT
IS TO BE,
IT IS
UP TO ME

"A soft answer turns away wrath, but a harsh word stirs up anger."
Proverbs 15:1 NKJV

Chapter 8

Growing up at Connie Maxwell And Loving It

Connie Maxwell, through God's love and grace, actually
threw me "the life line" and brought to me
a life of hope, survival, and opportunity.

A Brief Overview

What a beginning! My very early childhood years were filled
with many blessings and the love of a wonderful mother. Then,
my childhood was shattered by her death, the constant
shifting of a place to call home, and the frequent changing of
schools – in fact, four school changes by the second half of
the third grade.

I had just turned five years old when my mother died. She
was the victim of colon cancer at age forty-one – so young to
die and leave her family whom she loved so dearly. Following
the first year of her death, I remained at home with my
father and only sister. Then, it was off to my maternal
grandmother's home for the next two years. Oh, how I loved
Gran! She was just as wonderful and special to me as my
mother and she did such a good job of spoiling me and making
me feel really good about myself in those tender developing
years.

131

Again, trauma came. Gran died when I was only eight years old. What a void! I had now experienced the death of two of the closest people in my young life. I wondered, "Where to next?" To this day I remember that uncertainty and insecurity.

Next, I went to live with my aunt and uncle. This experience was very difficult for me, for by then I was so fragile and even more insecure. The toll of change had made an indelible imprint on my life! After six months, change was to come again – this time to Connie Maxwell Children's Home.

Glimpses into My Early Years and My Need for Connie Maxwell

Numerous flashbacks fill my early childhood memories of the various places I called home. Unfortunately, my father was a victim of alcoholism; however, he was never violent or abusive. When he was not drinking, he worked the farmland with the help of five older brothers. When he was drinking, often weeks at a time, my mother had to be mother and father, the homemaker, the farmer, and the caretaker of all of the family. My mothers and brothers had to "tend" the farm, harvesting the crops of cotton, soybeans, corn, and other vegetables. This had to be done when the crops were ready – certainly not when my father was sober enough to do the work. My mother still had numerous tasks to do. These were the years of absolutely no conveniences in the small rural community of Smoaks, located in Colleton County, South Carolina. My mother was compelled not only to grow the crops but also to harvest them and preserve the food for her family for the upcoming winter months. She, too, had to milk the cows, make all the clothes for the family, cook meals for nine people every day and keep clothes clean for the entire family. Just washing clothes was an ordeal in itself, with neither a washing machine nor indoor plumbing. Water had to be drawn from the well for the mounds of clothes that piled up each day, and these clothes had to be hung on clotheslines to dry. My only sister, Jeanette, who was ten years older than I, was a great help to my mother during her illness. Jeanette also helped to care for me while our mother was so ill. For the next year after our mother's death, Jeanette continued to provide care for me. This was her final year in high school. I went to school with Jeanette every day and sat in first and second grade classrooms. The teachers knew of my mother's illness and death and they welcomed me. They gave me "work" to do, so I had "kindergarten" some thirty years before public school kindergarten classes were available, and I learned from just listening to the lessons taught to others. Jeanette left to go to college the next fall.

The loss of our mother was very difficult for Jeanette. She suffered much pain and grief. I can remember her tears and sadness. We were close and I cried even more because Jeanette was so upset. I can remember with fondness my mother shelling field peas, snapping green beans – all in preparation for canning. There were no fans to cool her as she worked, but with so many depending on her, she had many things to do in our one-parent home. The love and concern she showed her family, and even many others, helped to compensate for the illness my dad had and the problems it caused our family.

My mother could have gone to college, as did her older brother. She was so smart. Instead, she chose to marry at age fifteen and then have her firstborn at age sixteen. While she obviously made a poor choice of a life's mate at that early age, motherhood to her was what life was all about. She was a wonderful mother to all of us over a twenty-year period of childbearing and then for five years after her last child. She gave birth to seven living children plus two "stillborn" babies.

My mother was very dedicated to her family. She was always at home with us, always available for our needs. She was a gentle, caring, and loving mother. She comforted and reassured us, helping to compensate for my dad's weakness.

My mother was also "the nurse" of our rural community. Although she did not finish high school and had no medical training, she studied and learned how to care for the sick. She ordered by mail books about childbirth, child care, various illnesses, and ways to heal wounds, burns, and fevers. To this day, I still have one of her medical books, copyrighted 1926. I treasure this book. It, to me, is a symbol of her desire to learn and to use this knowledge to love and care for others.

There were no antibiotics in my mother's day. There was no doctor within ten miles of our country home, so families with babies sick with colic, colds, coughs, and fevers and other illnesses came to her for help. She usually could make the most common ailments better. I think she must have used carborated ointment, salt, turpentine, and castor oil as healing agents. She also helped to deliver babies when the country doctor could not make it to the homes.

When did she find time to do all that she did? There was always time for those in need. She must have been exhausted everyday of her life. Her commitment to others set an example for me to follow. I believe my decision to enter nursing as a career was greatly influenced by my memories of my mother and her desire to help heal others. My desire to become a nurse could have been prompted by seeing my mother so very ill in her final days. Most probably the career decision I made came as the result of a combination of those two early observations of my mother, coupled later with lessons I learned while in the care of loving people at Connie Maxwell Children's Home.

In my mind's eye, I see my earliest of childhood homes. We had no heat in our home except in the room where the fireplace was located. This was actually the living room where we all gathered except to eat in the kitchen and to sleep in the bedrooms. I recall our moving my mother's sick bed into this room in the last couple of months of her life. I recall seeing her being moved by ambulance in December 1945 to the hospital where she later died. I know exactly where the ambulance parked and its direction in the yard. I still "see" her kissing each of us, and holding us close to her heart. I remember her tears and the handkerchief she used to cover most of her face. This was my last time to see her alive. It's a painful image. She wanted so much to stay home and care for her children, but God was calling her home. Somewhere I have read that God never takes anything from His children that He does not replace with something better. How could anything be better than my mother? What could replace her? Little did I know then, that God, too, had a plan for me. He would take care of me in a very special way and in a very special place, just as my mother had cared for and loved me in our home during those first five years of my life.

Still more flashbacks fill my mind's memory book. My next two years of living with Gran were very happy years. She cared for me deeply and loved me dearly. Wherever she went, I went,

too. How I remember trailing her among the flowers, and
through the vegetable garden, and among the hen sheds,
gathering eggs. She cooked everything I liked to eat. She was
filled with godly love and she shared it abundantly. She made
me feel so special in her attempt to fill the void created by my
mother's death. This newly found wonderful life was to be
interrupted again. Gran became ill and died very shortly
thereafter.

For the next six months, I lived in Walterboro with an Aunt
Eva and Uncle Jim – my mother's brother. My Uncle Jim, a
Wofford College graduate, gladly welcomed me into his home.
He especially exerted a most positive influence on my young
life. This, however, was marred by my Aunt Eva's negative
feelings toward my father. She thought my father should be
the one who should provide and care for me.

Aunt Eva and Uncle Jim were teachers in Charleston County
schools for more than thirty-five years. They commuted to
school from Walterboro each day, so someone had to be found
to keep me before and after school and sometimes during the
day, or I had to change schools and travel with them each day.
I changed schools again and enrolled in a Charleston school.

My Aunt Eva was quick to criticize me. She rarely
complimented me for anything. I worked hard to please her
with good grades earned at school. I attempted to help her
with little chores that I could manage in her home. Attempts
to please were often to no avail.

One day when my Uncle Jim was on a business trip, I was in the
kitchen with my Aunt Eva. She looked at me, called my name,
and said, "Your mother should never have had all those babies

to look after. You were born last. You could be the very cause of her death!" What a terrible thing for her to have said to me, an eight-year-old child already devastated by the loss of my mother and my grandmother. I can remember putting my head down, focusing my eyes on the floor, saying nothing and walking away from her. I wanted to get away to a far part of the yard. I found the shade of a persimmon tree and sat down under it. I felt horrible that I had caused my mother, whom I loved so much, to die. I cried and cried until my eyes were nearly swollen shut. My black and white spotted cat came and sat with me. He rubbed against me over and over again, climbed up into my lap and stayed a long time. That cat sensed that I was upset and something was terribly wrong. He stayed with me until I finally got enough courage to go back into the house sometime later. As I looked back even years later, I realized that Connie Maxwell was truly God's plan for me! It was a place of refuge, comfort, security, contentment and love. I thank God everyday for this blessing.

Arriving and Living at Connie Maxwell

It was December 29, 1948, just a little over three years since my mother's death and I was to face yet another change in my life. I remember that day so well. It was a bitterly cold and frightening day! How was I to know, at just eight years of age, that Connie Maxwell was my answer? How was I to understand that Connie Maxwell would become a place where I would be loved and cared for? After so much change, how could I readily understand that this new move would really be best for me? It's really hard to analyze life's experiences at such a young age, and it's even much harder when you are insecure, uncertain and feel unloved and unwanted. Connie Maxwell was to be the answer to the questions I had pondered. But I really didn't know it at the time.

Aunt Eva and Uncle Jim took me to Connie Maxwell Children's Home. It was such a long journey from Walterboro to Greenwood. I saw rolling hills and places that I had never seen before. The unfamiliar roads would surely lead me to an unfamiliar place with all new people there.

Upon my arrival at Connie Maxwell, I went straight to Eason Home. There I met my first wonderful cottage parent – Mrs. Eulalah McDonald. She welcomed me with loving arms, took me into the group and made me feel comfortable in my new fourth home in eight years. "Mrs. Mac," as all of us girls called her, began immediately to fulfill her responsibilities for my training, my development, and my care – just as my very own mother did. She taught me many lessons about life. Sometimes the discipline was demanding, but I soon loved my new home and my new family. I learned how to live compatibly with seventeen other girls at Eason Home.

Over the years I learned to love and respect "Mrs. Mac" greatly. She helped me to know what stability of a home meant. She taught me how to trust others. She worked on rebuilding my self-confidence, and she encouraged me to do well in school. "Mrs. Mac" expected me to do well and I figured I had better give it my best! She worked with me over an eight-year span. What a tremendous job she had to do, being a houseparent for eighteen girls. She must have been made of iron and steel but welded with love. She always remained calm in all situations and disciplined us according to "the rules of the house."

Most discipline was done in a manner where we were deprived of something we liked to do. Special activities, like going to a movie downtown, going swimming, or attending basketball games at the gym were taken away. The time passed slowly until we could participate again. We all soon learned that bad behavior was totally unacceptable. This discipline taught each of us valuable lessons. What we learned then became principles for a lifetime.

All the years under "Mrs. Mac's" care taught me character building traits, such as dependability, honesty, responsibility, moral integrity and a committed work ethic. "Mrs. Mac" was patient and kind to all of us and she loved us. I appreciate all the guidance, love, and support she provided for me. She helped me to find an answer to those questions I had asked on December 29, 1948.

About one and a half years before I graduated from high school there was another adventure and another move facing me. I had indeed learned to feel at home at Eason Home and was not seeking any change. Dr. Sam Smith, Superintendent, called me into his office one day. He told me that I had so much sunshine and brightness in my life. He commended me for my progress in adjusting to Connie Maxwell, and for my work all through school. Then he said to me, "I have a tremendous favor I want you to do for me. If you are not comfortable doing this, just tell me. I want you and another older girl, Maxene Bishop, from Martha Smith Home, to move to Durst Home and help with the younger girls there. There are some girls at Durst with many problems and you will be able to help them. You don't have to do anything except to move there with them, set a good example for them and help them with whatever problems they have. I truly believe you and

Maxene can help get the situation under control." I said, "Yes," to Dr. Smith. He had enough confidence and trust in me to ask me to do this task and I felt I should give it my best. There had been several short-term cottage parents at Durst during the previous year and this had created problems.

Off to Durst Home I went, living there for the remainder of my stay at Connie Maxwell. I did my best to show concern and love for the girls and to be there for them. It worked. Dr. Smith was right.

After several months' stay at Durst, Mrs. Bernice Hilton came to be our cottage parent. She was another wonderful person. She encouraged me to do my best in whatever I did. She continued to provide wise counsel and built on the foundation that "Mrs. Mac" had begun. Mrs. Hilton had a relaxed manner about her. The housework and cooking responsibilities always got finished, but maybe not the same day we had started them. She was one to brag about her girls to anyone who would listen. She took great pride in her work as a cottage parent. We all loved her.

During my Connie Maxwell years, I tried to do everything that I did to the best of my ability. I wanted praise and affirmation from my Connie Maxwell family, not from my biological family.

Time was drawing close to the big day of graduation from Greenwood High School. At age seventeen and a half I realized I had spent more than one half my life at Connie Maxwell. How I wanted to hold on to that safe protective haven and the dear friends I had made. I knew I would miss my beloved home at Connie Maxwell, but at the very same time

I knew that I had matured enough to leave "home" and take another step in my life. I had been accepted into Greenville General Hospital's School of Nursing with Furman University courses. These two schools provided many learning experiences that prepared me for the nursing profession. Indeed, Connie Maxwell had nurtured me, and prepared me to enter young adulthood.

I left Connie Maxwell to further my education, so very thankful to God for his plan for me. Again, those questions that I asked of myself on my first day at Connie Maxwell had been answered. Connie Maxwell will always live in my heart and mind forever!

Learning the Work Ethic at Connie Maxwell

I learned much about the importance of work at Connie Maxwell. My first job, at age eight, was to dust furniture in two living rooms each day. My second assignment was to sweep and keep clean the wrap-around porch at Eason Home. Then came the dining room chores – setting the tables, washing dishes and later helping to cook for a house of eighteen girls. This cooking was some chore, as we had to prepare a meal before school each day. During fifth and sixth grades I helped with the library on campus – mostly dusting books and shelves. Later in the high school years, I worked some in the boys' homes. I remember primarily the ironing of shirts. You can't imagine how many shirts per week had to be ironed for eighteen boys. This was in the days before any permanent-press fabrics were available, and one hundred percent cotton was the fabric most used. I learned to finish them pretty well, I thought. If the cottage parent thought the outcome was a bad job, we started over again with no questions asked.

We definitely learned the work ethic well. We were instructed that what we did should be done correctly, never stopping until the job was finished to exacting specifications. My work assignments also included a learning adventure in the campus sewing room. Among our work were the tasks of making curtains for the cottages and repairing torn clothes. It was amazing that the garments actually seemed pretty decent! Mrs. Strickland, who supervised our sewing, said the skirts looked fine to her, so unbelievably I did wear them.

School Clubs and Activities

During the elementary and middle school years, hardly any clubs or activities were available. There were, however, numerous athletic activities.
Basketball probably was the biggest sport. I did not participate much in sports, nor did I sing in the choir. However, I did take piano lessons for three years. It was difficult to practice piano at Eason Home due to many of the piano keys being totally silent keys. The piano was quite old and in serious need of repair.

At Greenwood High School I was somewhat more involved. I always enjoyed attending the football games and being there with friends. These were fun times. There was many clubs one could join in high school. I was a member of the Latin Club and the Home Economics Club. In my junior year I was tapped to be in the Beta Club and was elected to serve as vice president during my senior year. What a celebration to graduate successfully and achieve a major goal in my life!

Other Positive Influences in My Life

While at Connie Maxwell, many people influenced my life. Dr. Sam Smith especially influenced me. His strong integrity, humbleness, intellect, perception, and compassion could not have been surpassed by anyone. He was a godly gentleman. Since Dr. Smith had grown up at Connie Maxwell, he surely understood each one of us. He always found the time and energy to compliment a child for having done well in schoolwork and other activities. His kind manner and words had a positive impact on my very being. I believe Dr. Smith's care and love uplifted every Connie Maxwell child. I am truly thankful that our paths crossed. As a role model and father figure, he helped me to grow and develop and become confident. How fortunate we were!

Mr. George Teasley (another Connie Maxwell staff member) taught lessons I will always remember. He showed us that good sportsmanship is a necessity. It was important for our team to win the game, but we knew that how the game was played was equally as valuable – a life's lesson learned through daily activities on campus.

Miss Rebecca Johnson, my social worker, was always there for me. She helped me understand the realistic part of my needing to be at Connie Maxwell.

Through his example as our campus minister, Dr. John Murdock helped me understand the value of life and how to help others. At age eleven, I accepted Christ as my Savior and was baptized in Connie Maxwell Baptist Church. Until this very day, those early days at Connie Maxwell Baptist under gird my Christian faith and desire to be active in church.

Others at Connie Maxwell, just too numerous to name, helped make me what I am. Included among these people were G. A. leaders, Sunday school teachers, and campus school teachers. All reflected God's love through the compassionate care they provided daily.

Family Visits

While at Connie Maxwell my biological family support was quite limited. Visits were few and far apart. My dad's only visit was to attend my graduation from Greenwood High School. During the nine and one half years that I lived at Connie Maxwell, I always wondered why he did not visit. I think it bothered him to know that I needed to live away from home, and possibly this made it too difficult for him to visit me.

My Aunt Eva and Uncle Jim who placed me at Connie Maxwell visited me about twice a year. After his death, my Aunt Eva usually came to see me on her way to visit other family members. My sister who was in college some of the years while I was at Connie Maxwell did not have a car, but she did visit when she could – about two or three times a year.

In most summers I visited with my family during our month's vacation. I saw my dad, my aunt, and my sister and later her family. Occasionally, I visited with a brother and his wife.

Later Connections with Family

Following my graduation from nursing school, I married a wonderful supportive husband and established a stable home. I visited my dad, sister and aunt periodically as I understood the value of family connections, which I had missed so much as a child and teenager. My dad spent six months of the last year of his life in my home in Anderson where Jim, my husband, and I lived at the time. I provided care and love for him. This was the longest time that he and I had spent together since I was six years old – some 24 years earlier. Dad died in 1970 from coronary artery disease.

Aunt Eva, after retiring from teaching in Charleston, moved to Anderson. I spent years assisting her, especially in getting her medical care and attending many of her other personal needs. I made it a point to see that she was never alone at holiday times. I remember these as lonely times as I grew up and with no one from my family visiting me regularly.

My sister and her family lived in Columbia. Since my Connie Maxwell years, I have continued to visit with her the most. I have attempted to help her when she needed support and love. I often helped her with her four children who are now grown. Jeanette is now confined to a nursing home, depending greatly on my moral support, mail, and telephone calls, little gifts and frequent and personal visits.

Mrs. Hilton, my second cottage parent, retired from Connie Maxwell, and moved to Columbia to live near a family member. Jim and I lived in Columbia too in the early sixties. Medicare was not available then. I worked as a registered nurse for an internist. I told Dr. Ben Miller about the common bond between Mrs. Hilton and me. He provided free medical care for her during the years until Medicare became available. That is the least I could do for her. It was a way to say thank you for all she had done for me in the earlier years. This was a special connection in my extended family.

Packing Suitcases: What a Memory!

Packing a suitcase or a piece of luggage for a trip is a difficult task for me. In my earlier years, I had to pack a suitcase and stay with a neighbor while my mother was ill. I had to pack to go to Gran's house to live. Even later packing a suitcase was necessary to go to live with my aunt and uncle. Next came the suitcase packing required to leave my familiar surroundings and move to Connie Maxwell. This particular packing of my few belongings proved to be the best move I had ever made. During the summers I packed to go see my family, then I packed to go back to Connie Maxwell after each visit. At age fifteen and a half, I packed a suitcase and moved from Eason Home to Durst Home. Two years later I had to pack a suitcase to go away to Greenville General School of Nursing and Furman University. Every one of these occasions that called for suitcase packing from ages four to seventeen years brought even more uncertainties into my life.

Even today when Jim and I are going on a pleasure trip I always attend to every detail, like stopping the mail and newspapers before packing. I delay the packing as long as I can.

The pain I felt in packing to leave my first wonderful home still lingers in my mind. Surely I'll overcome this bothersome task, and enjoy packing ""when I grow up."

Unforgettable Lessons Learned at Connie Maxwell

During my Connie Maxwell years, I learned lessons that still continue to strengthen and enrich my life. Above all, I learned that God' boundless love and abundant grace were always available and brought sustaining power in both the good times and the bad times.

I learned that God always provided for his children, even when families fell apart. Indeed, Psalm 27:10 and Psalm 68:4-6 has special meaning to me because of my Connie Maxwell experiences. I learned that Connie Maxwell's love and support were vital to my survival and to thousands of children from dysfunctional families over the many years at Connie Maxwell's history. I learned that good strong role models were vital to building integrity and character. I had such exemplary role models in my cottage parents, in Dr. Smith, and others. What wonderful gifts God gave to me!

I learned that work was honorable and that one was expected to do his or her best in everything. Moreover, I learned that a strong work ethic led to success. I learned never to feel sorry for myself, but to seize the opportunities I had and continue to strive for excellence.

I learned to constantly thank God for connecting Connie Maxwell and me. The rays of sunshine over those nine and one half years of living there brought joy and happiness. These have been the foundation for my commitment in my adult roles as wife, mother, nurse, church member, civic leader, and dedicated member of the Connie Maxwell Board of Trustees for ten years and the Conway Hospital Board of Trustees for four years.

What powerful lessons I learned while in the tender, caring, Christian ministry of Connie Maxwell Children's Home.

Special Thoughts and Ideas Worth Sharing with Today's Children

Generations have passed since Connie Maxwell opened its doors in 1892 to care for hurting children and youth. Needs have been served in so many ways, and with each decade new challenges have emerged. I have observed that today's children and youth have experienced some of the most complex problems of all times. Consequently, child care provisions have had to change to better serve these children. Certainly no group of children today could grow up as I did, but experiences and lessons of yesteryear provoke me to ask, "What information should or could I share that might benefit Connie Maxwell children today?"

To begin, I must tell children that life is not always fair, that life can be made more complicated by families that experience problems, and that sometimes children have the right to feel like nothing will ever turn out right for them. But I would assure them that with God's love and mercy, problems can be resolved and life can be better. Hope can be restored and good things will come to those who love the Lord and try to help themselves. I know; it happened for me.

I would tell the children that adversity and "hard times" toughen the spirit, challenge the mind, and make the child more resilient. This resilience develops determination and leads to success. And we know that success leads to success. Just look at the many successful men and women today who had a "new start" at Connie Maxwell.

I would tell the children that it is not Connie Maxwell's fault that they are there. Their presence at Connie Maxwell came as a result of death, illness, unfortunate circumstances, and problems in families and the inability of adults to deal with these problems effectively and still care for children at home. Regardless of the reason for placement at Connie Maxwell, there is an opportunity for a better life.

I would stress the fact that yesterday's children and today's children have a common link. Each of us needed a place to belong and to feel loved. Connie Maxwell has been and is that place.

My counsel of today's children at Connie Maxwell would be simple: Connie Maxwell is there for you – to nurture, to rebuild, and to restore. Connie Maxwell will make a difference. It is a home away from home, a family away from family, a place of peace rather than strife, and finally an opportunity for a lifetime rather than a stumbling block for failure.

Finally, I would remind today's children that God's love and grace can nurture one anywhere, but at Connie Maxwell and in its Christian family atmosphere, God can and will seem even more real and close. I know, I experienced this in my stay there. I would emphasize that we must know Him, seek Him, and follow Him even in the roughest times in growing up. Good things can and will happen. Everyone can be a winner. Trust Him and go for the good life!

A Child's Resilience and Connie Maxwell's Impact

A child's resilience – "Where does it come from?" – I often ponder. Did he or she get it through heredity, one's "deck of cards," or did the kindness, love, compassion of those who nurtured the child so early in life shape his or her very own being? As I reflect on life's experiences, study about children, and seek to help them through my commitment to my family, my church and Connie Maxwell, I now know that those who cared so much made all the difference.

After a child has experienced sadness, rejection and loneliness within a dysfunctional family for whatever reason, what causes him or her to bounce back? Adversity in a child's life can cripple temporarily, but adversity can be a catalyst for new beginnings and accomplishments.

Connie Maxwell's commitment is and has been to take the child, nurture the child, and offer hope and a support system that will bring healing. The good role models and the family atmosphere provided at Connie Maxwell have proven successful in restoring broken lives. I know; I have been there.

An Alumna's Reflections of Gratitude

As I conclude, I want to reflect just briefly on the magnificent beauty of what God has done for my life through the tender care, abundant love, and constant nurturing afforded me at a place I love to call home -- Connie Maxwell.

Above all, I am deeply grateful to God for the opportunities I had at Connie Maxwell. These opportunities allowed me to overcome fear and insecurity and to grow and develop positively in a Christian environment. Those nine and one-half special years helped me to become an adult molded with love and embraced by the Connie Maxwell family.

I want my daily work and my everyday life to reflect the values, morals, and integrity that were instilled in my by so many God-like people. It is my hope that facets of light from my actions everyday will reflect what I learned and what God made possible for me to experience beginning December 29, 1948.

I most sincerely want the Connie Maxwell legacy to be alive, vibrant, and growing through the Connie Maxwell Alumni Association. After all, we are the best testaments of the work at Connie Maxwell.

I most graciously thank every South Carolina Baptist and any other individual contributors for their belief in others, their desire to support little children and youth, and their commitment to further a cause initiated in 1892 by Dr. John C. Maxwell in memory of his own very young child – Connie. It is humbling to see the record – 108 years of service – and then to see the product – thousands of lives cultivated through a dedicated ministry to children. Join me in remembering and celebrating what God has done for so many deserving children.

-----Nora Dean Padgett Mahaffey

"Whoever welcomes one of these little children in my name welcomes me; and whoever welcomes me does not welcome me but the one who sent me."
Mark 9:37 NIV

Author's commentary: Dean's life story and comments about Connie Maxwell served to deepen my faith not only in her, but in the reality that Connie Maxwell and its staff has played such a significant role in shaping the lives of many, many, many young boys and girls.

Her husband, Jim, is much like my wife, Pat. I think Jim Mahaffey loves Connie Maxwell almost as much as Dean does.

Dean has never let adversity keep her from doing what she knew was the right thing to do. Her life's story made me realize how much she has continued to practice what she learned at Connie Maxwell. Her actions make her one of the most outstanding role models we have today.

She is currently (2000) the president of the Connie Maxwell Alumni Association where she has, also, served on the Board of Directors for many years.

AND REMEMBER,

IF IT
IS TO BE,
IT IS
UP TO ME

"The Lord, the Lord God, merciful and gracious, long-suffering, and abounding in goodness and truth..."
Exodus 34:6 NKJV

SOMEONE TO COUNT ON

Chapter 9

The events that caused this chapter to be added to this book, made me realize, as I have several times during its writing, that something almost miraculous has been at work.

On Saturday, September 9, 2000, my wife, Pat and I were shopping at our local supermarket. Pat happened to see a magazine at the checkout counter, *"Women's World."* She had never purchased a copy before and could not later explain why she bought one on this particular day.

She brought the copy home and late on Saturday night, as she flipped through the pages of the magazine, she saw an article written by Taryn Phillips-Quinn entitled, "Someone To Count On." It was a short story about Angelia Faith (Belcher) McCalla and how she met her "guardian angel," Doris. With great surprise and joy she awoke me from my newly found sleep to tell me that we had to add another chapter to our book.

I was scheduled to have the manuscript of this book at the printers by September 12, 2000. I made several telephone calls to determine if I could add another chapter; what were the legal ramifications of using the article in its entirety; and could we reschedule printing time, etc.

I first got in touch with Angie to get her permission. She was pleased to be part of the effort and gave her O.K. to proceed. She also gave me the telephone number for Taryn Phillips-Quinn who had authored the article.

When I spoke to Taryn she indicated she would need to obtain permission from her editor-in-chief, Stephanie Saible. All of this happened on Monday, September 11, 2000. I conveyed my concern to Taryn regarding the deadline I was working under and she pulled out all stops in order for permission to be granted. September 12, 2000 I received the permission to use the article exactly as Taryn had written it for *"Woman's World"* in the September 12, 2000 issue.

The following therefore is used by permission from *Woman's World* - The Woman's Weekly, Heinrich Bauer North America, Inc., 270 Sylvan Avenue, Englewood Cliffs, NJ 07632 as written by Taryn Phillips-Quinn, Articles editor, "My Guardian Angel" and titled, "Someone To Count On."

"When she arrived at the Connie Maxwell Children's Home, all Angelia McCalla wanted was a safe place to grow up. She found that and more, thanks to an angel named Doris."

"With a ring of the bell, school ended, and my classmates raced for home—and the hugs, kisses, cookies and milk I imagined waiting for them there. I lagged behind. Home was the last place I wanted to be.

"I never knew what to expect when I opened the door. Would Mom be sad and crying? Or would she be too numb from medication to realize I'd walked in?

"At 12, I was living with a shadow over my life, and it blotted out any chance I had of feeling happy or safe. What I didn't know was that soon I'd meet a guardian angel who would take me under her wing, and with her love and guidance, I'd find the happiness I longed for...

"Until I was five, I had a happy life with my parents. Then, suddenly, Dad left. Mom was devastated, and as time passed, she slipped into depression.

"Later, I learned that she had been diagnosed with bi-polar disorder, a chemical imbalance that causes mood swings, but all I knew then was that she cried and was sad all the time. She was given medication, but it made her so lifeless that she found it hard to work or take care of me. I'd often have to put myself to bed at night, hungry and without a bath. Doesn't she know I'm here? I'd quietly weep.

"We were so poor that I never had enough to eat, and my clothes were shabby. "Hey, bow-wow," the kids at school would taunt. "You're dirty!"

"I'm just a nobody! I'd cry in humiliation.

"My feelings of worthlesssness made it hard for me to concentrate in school, and my report cards were filled with Ds. I'm stupid! I'd cry. I wish I were dead!

"But something inside me wouldn't let me give up. There has to be a better life! I thought.

"Yet my self-esteem was so low that I didn't think anyone cared about what happened to me. Then when I was 13, someone from my church told me about the Connie Maxwell Children's home, an orphanage for children who didn't have parents, or whose parents couldn't take care of them.

Suddenly, I felt a stirring of hope. It has to be better than home, I thought sadly.

"She took me to talk to our minister. When he explained that the kids at Connie Maxwell lived in a "cottage" with a housemother who fixed their meals and made sure they had clean clothes, I thought, It sounds like Heaven!

"Wanting the best for me, Mom gave her permission. A week later, a social worker drove me to my new home. As we entered the campus of brick houses on tree-lined streets, I worried, Will I fit in?

"Then I met my house mother, Doris. Instead of the warm greeting I had hoped for, Doris told me, "You're going to have to follow the rules."

"My heart sank. She didn't seem very motherly.

"But I wasn't disappointed when I saw the room I'd share with another girl. It was plain, but there was a desk where I could do my homework. Filling with peace, I prayed, Thank You!

"Still, whenever I thought of Mom, I'd wonder, Does she miss me? She'd call, but she was never well enough to visit.

""She's doing the best she can." Doris would soothe. 'You have to make a life for yourself."

"You don't understand! I wanted to cry.

"But looking back, she saw what I *really* needed, and that was to believe in myself. Doris guided me, pushing me and pulling me back when I needed that, too. Even if she didn't shower me with hugs and kisses, she showed her love in a million ways. I learned to read it in the way her face lit up when I came home from school, in the warmth in her voice when she sat talking, and her cool hand on my forehead when I felt feverish. She made me feel that I was worth caring about.

"I'd never owned new clothes, but soon after I arrived, Doris took me shopping. I didn't even know what to choose, but Doris smiled, "You're going to have to learn to dress like a young girl." When she pulled out a pair of polka dot shorts and a cute blouse, I was thrilled.

"Doris made sure we always had plenty to eat. "Have seconds," she'd encourage—and I would. And when she made my favorite meal—roast beef with potatoes—she'd let me have a little taste before supper. I'd never felt so special.

"But I still felt like a nobody. Unsure of myself, I struggled at school. "Just do your best," Doris encouraged. I felt my heart tug. She sounded just like . . . a mother.

"But I thought doing my best meant being perfect.

"As one year passed, then two, I studied hard, and by age 15, I was a straight A student. Still, I feared failure. I studied until late very night. Hoping to gain acceptance, I joined clubs, and because I was good at art, I never said no when someone asked if I would make invitations or paint pictures for them.

"One day, Doris told me, "I'm worried about you."

""Why?" I wondered.

""You're doing too much," she explained softly. "People will still like you if you don't get perfect grades, or if you say no."

"But I didn't believe her. So Doris got tough. "Lights out," she'd say when I'd study past bedtime. When she limited my activities, I fumed, "You're mean!"

"But I had to follow her rules. And to my surprise, it didn't matter to the people who liked me if I said no. I began to trust Doris—and to believe in myself.

"At 19, friends and teachers urged me to enter our high school beauty pageant. I didn't think I was good enough to win, but Doris encouraged, "You'll never know if you don't try." When I entered—and won—she was elated.

""You did it!" she cheered. I felt a surge of happiness, and in that moment, I realized that Doris truly loved me, and I loved her.

"When I graduated from high school, Doris cried tears of joy when I received my diploma. I was happy, but sad, too, because I'd be going to college and living in a dorm. I thought Doris and I would have to say goodbye. Then she told me, "You could live in the house I own in town. I need someone to help me take care of it."

"My heart filled with love. "You can count on me," I smiled. And to myself I added, Just the way I've been able to count on you.

"And as the years passed, Doris shared all my milestones: college graduation, my first job, my wedding to Brian. And five months ago when I learned I was expecting, Doris was ecstatic.

"Doris is retired now, and we see each other often. Each time we say goodbye, she says three little words that mean the world to me: "I love you."

"Doris will always hold a special place in my heart. She gave me a mother's love when I needed it, but more, she taught me to believe in myself.

"I'm 24 now, and my life has turned out so much better than I dreamed possible. Sometimes when I wake up in the morning, I wonder if it's all a dream. Then I see Brian, and I feel my baby's kicks. Thanks to Doris, I found my happy ending.

--as told to
Taryn Phillips-Quinn

Author's Commentary: Angie (Belcher) McCalla is an excellent example of what can happen when we let our attitude be guided by and patterned after God's love and concern. Angie has proven that not only can you climb out of the depths of despair, but also you can become a "role model" for others to follow. Angie is indeed a "role model." Thanks again, Angie, for giving all of us an example to follow.

WE CANNOT HOLD A TORCH TO ANOTHER'S PATH WITHOUT BRIGHTENING OUR OWN."
--Ben Sweetland

"Be still, and know that I am God; I will be exalted among the nations, I will be exalted in the earth."

Psalm 46:10 NKJV

Chapter 10

A MAN ALL WRAPPED UP IN HIMSELF MAKES
A MIGHTY SMALL PACKAGE

I wondered how I would ever start writing this book and where I would get most of the material. I had several conferences with my mentor and dear friend, Mack Baltzegar. He suggested I write out a list of questions and send them to Connie Maxwell alumni that might be interested in telling me about their lives before, during and after their Connie Maxwell stay. Some responded and some did not. I will forever be grateful to those alumni who responded to the questionnaire. Thank you a thousand times. Your stories make me realize how much we have in common.

****

Personal Story - Betty Taylor

What were the circumstances that brought you to Connie Maxwell?

My father drank a lot. He and my mother were separated and I had a little sister. My dad had a brother living with us who did the cooking. He also drank quite a lot. A lady in one of the churches and a doctor contacted Connie Maxwell and they decided two little girls should not be living like that, so Connie Maxwell became our home.

What are some positive experiences that you had to Connie Maxwell?

Having a Christmas tree for the first time. Attending church. Teaching Sunday school.

Explain some things that happened to you that brought you success because of what you learned or experienced at Connie Maxwell.

Managing my time. Making time to do lots of things. Handling money. Making it go as far as possible.

How was your cottage mother an influence (negative or positive) on you?

Mrs. Bessie Upton was the kind of lady I wanted to be. She cared for us as a mother. Even when we were punished, we knew we were loved and cared about. She trusted us and allowed us to do things on our own.

What are your thoughts about campus work --- good or bad?

Worked in sewing room (Mrs. Rose). Worked at storeroom (Mr. Blackwell). Worked at cold storage (Mr. Blackwell).

I think working in the different homes, cooking, and cleaning has really helped me learn how to budget my time, cook well and save money. Getting paid our senior year made it possible for me to save money when I thought it would be impossible. I, later, saved enough in seventeen years to pay cash for a three bedroom brick home and eleven acres of land. Cooking and learning how to cook made it possible to prepare foods "good and tasty" and still save money. In turn, I have tried to teach these things to my children.

How are things you learned at Connie Maxwell still shaping your life today?

This was an interesting question. Everyday lots of things I do or start to do make me remember my years at Connie Maxwell. At work I'm not late and I get more work done than most, as I know how to do lots of things at the same time. I also try to make some one that is not feeling just right, feel better.

What advice would you have for children that are at Connie Maxwell now?

Stay there as long as you can and learn all you can. Put what you learn (from books and experience) to use in your life everyday. Just because you have a "place" to go, don't let it influence you to leave if deep down you know it is not the best for you.

What adjustments have you made (if any) when you are asked, "Where were you raised?

I made no adjustments except to talk more about Connie Maxwell. I never miss an opportunity to let anyone know where I was raised and how proud I am of Connie Maxwell.

--Betty Taylor

****

Personal Story - Charles Robinson

What were some of the circumstances that brought you to Connie Maxwell?

My mother and father separated when I was two years old. It was very difficult then, as it is today, for a single mother to raise children. I don't know how the social worker (Mrs. Taggart) found out about us. The next thing I knew we were on our way to the Connie Maxwell Orphanage in 1943. The people at Connie Maxwell are responsible for me being the man I am today.

What are some positive experiences that you had at Connie Maxwell?

1. Accepting Jesus Christ as my personal Lord and Savior.
2. Learning to be honest and truthful in all dealings.
3. Playing baseball, football and basketball.
4. Mountain cottage with the river and lake.
5. Camp Rawls. I was star camper in 1945.
6. Making lifelong friends.
7. Rooming with a great guy named Billy Daniels.

Name two or three staff members that had a very special impact on shaping your life and character at Connie Maxwell.

Dr. Sam Smith – our leader, Dr. John Murdock – our minister, Dick Rhodes – dairy farm, Bill Clyburn – truck farm, and L. S. Adams – maintenance.

Explain some things that happened to you that brought you success because of what you learned or experienced at Connie Maxwell:

- Being competitive in sports. This carries over into the work place.
- Strong work habits.
- Strong work ethics.
- Learning to always tell the truth and be honest in whatever you do.

How was your cottage mother an influence (negative or positive) on you?

Mrs. N. G. Ballenger (wife of a deceased Methodist minister) taught me to always be honest and tell the truth. She said to me, "if you always tell the truth you will never have to hang your head in shame." What a wonderful lady she was. Mrs. W. Sam Vaughn from over in Jonesville, SC was our cook. She was another wonderful lady.

What were some things you did in your free time on campus --- go to town, go to movies, work, play, etc.?

Went to the movies on Saturday. Admission was nine cents at the State Theater.

Once Tex Ritter came to the theater with his big white horse. What a thrill for a kid to see a western movie star in person walking his horse up and down the aisle.

Most of my free time was devoted to practicing for each sport.

How are things you learned at Connie Maxwell still shaping your life today?

- Being able to mingle well with people.
- Learning to be honest and truthful.
- Developing strong moral character.
- Strong work habits.
- Strong work ethics.

Did you go to college when you left Connie Maxwell? Did Connie Maxwell help you financially?

I graduated from Furman University in 1955. I did receive financial aid from Connie Maxwell. I also had a partial baseball scholarship. Played baseball three years. Also, I was the athletic trainer to the football team. In 1954 I was selected as one of the trainers to the South Carolina-North Carolina High School Shrine Bowl football game.

What advice would you have for children that are at Connie Maxwell now?

Accept Jesus Christ as personal Lord and Savior.
Always be honest in everything you do and tell the truth.
Learn good work habits and ethics. I believe the highest compliment a person can receive is when someone says about you --- There is a young man or young lady of integrity.

What adjustments have you made (if any) when you are asked, "Where were you raised?"

I have never been asked, "where were you raised?" I have told many people voluntarily that I grew up at the Connie Maxwell Children's Home in Greenwood, SC.

--Charles Robinson

****

Personal Story - Harold Diggers

What were the circumstances that brought you to Connie Maxwell?

There were ten children. My mother died of cancer in the late forties. My Dad's only occupation was as a sharecropping farmer. After my mom's death, my dad, still being a young man, commenced doing what young men do, find companionship. Needless to say, that left his children in need.

What were some negative experiences that happened at Connie Maxwell?

Naturally when I arrived there I was in shock. I was assigned to Convention Building. There must have been eighteen young boys, plus the cottage parents, standing on the front porch to greet my younger brother, Kenzie and me. We were separated from our four sisters, the oldest being Grace and Cindy and the youngest being Faye and Judy. At this time I had no idea where they had gone.

What were some positive experiences that you had at Connie Maxwell?

I cannot name the numerous positive experiences. There are too many. I will name just a few: coon hunting; brews; working on the farm; plowing fields with tractors; doing the farm work with other boys; having the run of so many acres; checking cows and horses; unloading box cars of produce; being called out at night to unload produce from trucks; being taken out of school to process corn and gather vegetables; and working with people such as Doc Rhodes, Mr. Clyburn and others which allowed me to grow, mature and assume responsibilities. I could go on forever because my positive experiences are too many.

Name two or three staff members that had a very special impact on shaping your life and character at Connie Maxwell.

Dr. Sam Smith had a great influence on my life at Connie Maxwell and on my life today. However, there are several people who have influenced my life in a greater degree. I will list them: Mrs. Alma Vincent, cottage mother at Ellenberg. Her acceptance of me I cannot explain. Mr. Doc Rhodes and Mr. Clyburn were farm superintendents. Their confidence in me built my self-esteem and my confidence. As a young child at Convention home, Pop Linler was also a great influence.

Explain some things that happened to you that brought you success because of what you learned or experienced at Connie Maxwell.

Each one of us was required to perform a certain job at Connie Maxwell. We worked in our campus home as a young student. After reaching the age of twelve as a boy in my case, you were sent to the farms. Under the supervision of a farm superintendent you learned discipline, time management, use of tools, teamwork, confidence, and comradeship. Work at Connie Maxwell back in the early fifties was a necessity for us to survive. As young boys doing our daily chores we knew it was a necessity. In most cases, we performed our duties diligently, and in my opinion, the training we received and the guidance we were given has helped me to provide for my family and myself.

Did you work on the farm and what are your thoughts about campus work --- good or bad?

Upon turning twelve years old, I was assigned the job of "gym boy" in our old gym. After three months I was transferred to the vegetable farm with Mr. Clyburn. Here I worked for the next three and one half years. Then I requested a transfer to the cattle farm. There I worked for approximately the next six years.

I think this campus work was the best experience and training I could have received. All through the years of raising my two boys to adulthood, I have often wished they could have known the experiences and the comradeship we shared on the farms.

What were some things you did in your free time on campus --- go to town, go to movies, work, play etc.?

For the most part Saturday after 12:00 and Sunday, was considered free time. Ninety percent of my Saturday afternoons were spent doing extra work on the farms for twenty-five cents per hour. Of course some of those Saturdays were spent for disciplinary reasons. Every Sunday evening for about six years straight I would work extra after church on the cattle farm feeding and checking cows. This way I could make enough money to purchase a Pepsi Cola, a Baby Ruth candy bar and a pack of Winston cigarettes and still have two or three dollars to give my sister, Faye for her personal needs.

How are the things you learned at Connie Maxwell still shaping your life today?

Patience, ability to communicate, waiting your turn, sharing. I could list many, many more, but I would like to say this – we were taught discipline, good work habits, and responsibility to our jobs and for one another. From this came confidence that I could take care of myself after leaving Connie Maxwell. At present I have a wife of twenty-five years, have reared two boys, and never accepted a penny of supplement from any one or any organizations. I have always paid and earned my way. This I owe to what I learned at Connie Maxwell.

What advice would you have for children that are at Connie Maxwell now?

Gene, this is a hard one. The situation at Connie Maxwell today, I am sad to say, I do not know much about. It is certainly much different from what we experienced. I would say this; resist adoption, resist foster care, and resist the return to an abusive environment. Try to remain at Connie Maxwell until graduation for all the benefits I have previously mentioned.

What adjustments have you made (if any) when you are asked, "Where were you raised?"

I do not hesitate, I will say immediately "I was raised at Connie Maxwell Children's Home in Greenwood, SC." I do not seek any kind of benefits nor sympathy. I am proud to be an alumnus of Connie Maxwell.

--Harold Driggers

****

Personal Story Linnie Edenfield

What were some of the circumstances that brought you to Connie Maxwell?

My name is Linnie Sweat Edenfield. When I was nine years old my mother died from urinal poison. She was a young mother of twelve and she had been sick for a long time. I, Linnie, was the oldest girl and after mom passed away, I was pretty much responsible for my four younger siblings. My father never recovered from my mother's death and we were pretty much left on our own. My grandmother found us and put some of us with relatives. My sister, Edie went to stay with a friend of my aunt. After about ten months of going from place to place, Doug, Edie and myself were sent to Connie Maxwell and Jerry and Betty came after they had their sixth birthday. We were very afraid, away from our brothers and sisters, and not knowing what was going to happen to us. Needless to say we did not adjust well at first. Doug and Edie and I were isolated from the rest of the children for about ten days. No one explained what was going on and we did not leave the room

171

even to go to the dinning room to eat. To this day I do not know why we were treated this way as I never knew of any other new kids having to do this.

What were some positive experiences that you had at Connie Maxwell?

There are many positive things that I could mention. First, I had many advantages that I would not have had if I had not been at Connie Maxwell. I loved the yearly trips we took to the mountains while I was younger. I loved the new pool and was one of the first lifeguards for the girls. As I grew older I was allowed to go off campus and work in the summer. When I graduated I did not have to worry about funds to go to school. Connie Maxwell paid half my tuition. After I married, I repaid the loan. I had wonderful friends, learned some wonderful life lessons, and made the best housekeeper you would ever want to meet. I'm not a good seamstress but I can cook up a storm.

Name two or three staff members that had a very special impact on shaping your life and character at Connie Maxwell.

Every staff member had a part in shaping my life and character. Whether we realized it or not, we watched and learned from the staff as well as the other children. I must say that my cottage mothers had the most influence on shaping my life. From some I learned it didn't matter where you came from, you were worth loving. From others I learned that you had to work extra hard to please. From Ms. Upton I learned what it was to be really loved. She taught me to laugh when I got frustrated instead of lashing out in anger. From

"Dr. Sam" I learned that I was worth more than I thought I was and I could do anything if I worked hard at it.

Explain some things that happened to you that brought you success because of what you learned or experienced at Connie Maxwell.

This is a hard question for me because I have had so much success. I attribute all of it to past experiences at Connie Maxwell. I have worked hard and that is because I was taught to do so when I was a student at Connie Maxwell. I have not had one success that is big but all of them were because of what I learned there.

Did you play sports at Connie Maxwell? What were they – How did they influence you while at Connie Maxwell and/or after you left Connie Maxwell?

I played every sport that was in season at the time. I have to say my favorite was basketball. Basketball made me known on campus and gave me some measure of celebrity status. Basketball is a team sport. I learned quickly that if you didn't play as a team you would lose. When I played basketball we were only allowed to dribble twice and played only half of the court. Let's face it, you don't get very far on two dribbles. After I left Connie Maxwell my basketball days were over and I took up hockey. Believe me basketball is a lot safer than hockey. After I married I played basketball for one season and found that I really didn't know how to play, especially with tough Army women. We lost every game we played.

Did you work on the farm, sewing room, print shop, lunchroom, etc., and what are your thoughts about campus work - Good or bad?

I worked in the lunchroom and it was O.K. I think that campus work was very positive except when it was the only thing you did. Working made you more aware of your surroundings. You learned to do a good job or else. I would say campus work was very positive and should be re-implemented.

How are the things you learned at Connie Maxwell still shaping you life?

While at Connie Maxwell I learned to be truthful, of high moral standard, and not afraid or ashamed of admitting I did not know everything. Those truths are mine today. I tried very hard to instill them in my children and I am seeing them in my grandchildren today. I also learned to give an honest days work for my dollar and continue to do that today. One truth I learned continues to shape my life. If I expect to do anything worthwhile I had better have a helper that is perfect and makes no mistakes. My Lord Jesus continues to be my helper and as I get older I lean on Him more and more.

What advice would you have for children that are at Connie Maxwell now?

There is so much I could say here; however, my advice is that the situation is not as bad as it first appears. Sure you are separated from your family and that makes you sad. It is much better to use the circumstances to your advantage instead of working against them. Be very patient, wait, and use every opportunity to better your circumstances. Choose

174

yourself a good role model and go from there. Only you are responsible for how you behave and how you behave makes it either easier or harder, the choice is yours.

What adjustments have you made (if any) when you are asked, "where were you raised?"

I have always found that when I say I grew up at Connie Maxwell it leads to questions about the home and about myself. I have a great love and respect for Connie Maxwell and have no problem saying I grew up there and feel very privileged to have done so.

A Final Note

I would like to add a little footnote about my family. I married a wonderful man, Al, who was in the Air Force. We traveled much of the United States and saw a great deal of Europe as well as the Orient. Al had two tours where I was not allowed to travel with him. We had a son, Jim, and a daughter, Kim. Al finished his tour in the Air Force when Jim entered his first year at Clemson. We live in Lexington, SC, very content with each other after forty-four years. We have four granddaughters, Erin, Anna, Caitlin and Mariah and two grandsons, Jacob and Kellen. All of them are beautiful and very bright.

--Linnie Sweat Edenfield

****

Personal Story - Joe Taylor

What were some of the circumstances that brought you to Connie Maxwell?

My grandmother, Ora (Granny) Blalock, raised me in the city of Belton, SC. She was a native of Wilberton, Okla. and part Choctaw Indian. Her husband had worked most of his life in the coal mines. He died at a young age from "black lung disease." Ora heard about the great cotton explosion in the southern states and thought it a good idea to bring her family there and try their fortunes. She had a family of four at the time consisting of two boys and two girls. Edith was her baby and my mother. Sally was the eldest daughter and my aunt. She settled in a small town not to far from Belton, called Honea Path, SC. My mother worked in the Belton cotton mill and could barley support her family. Child care centers were virtually unheard of in those days so Granny was given the task of baby sitting me which meant that there was only one "bread winner" and that was my Mother. She only earned eleven cents per hour in those days. Needless to say food was very scarce. We lived in a company house and bought our food from the company store. And this is really the only way that we were able to live. In 1939, my Granny got pneumonia and died a short time thereafter. My Mother's grief was beyond belief. She soon lost her job and we were on the welfare rolls. She began to drink excessively and I began to run around all over the neighborhood doing just as I pleased. My behavior got the attention of the welfare agency and thus my processing for Connie Maxwell Orphanage was underway. In late 1939, I arrived at Connie Maxwell Orphanage on a cold rainy afternoon in November and started my career as an Orphan. In all my memories this was, and still is, the saddest day of my life. I

176

felt as if no one on planet earth wanted me, a little boy of only five years old. What had I done to deserve such an outcome. Had I known God then I probably would have cursed Him. However, I now know that God loves little five-year old boys. Praise His wonderful name!

Upon my arrival at Connie Maxwell, I was assigned to Greenwood Cottage (number one, as we knew it.) Boy, you talk about a house full of kids—we really had one. There were three huge bedrooms and more than forty children. Here is my negative---the housemother was fortunate if she even saw all the boys in a twenty-four hour period. She obviously had very little time for petting. Sometimes she would not confront you during a whole day.

Saturday night was fight night. Little boys fought little boys and middle size boys fought their size while the BIG boys looked on and whooped and hollered. And if they did not like the way you fought they took it out on your backside. You really wanted to grow-up fast in those days. Lastly, Christmas meant very little in those days. One year I got one present only and it was marked for a boy of twelve.

In 1946, an evangelist, whose name I cannot remember came to the home and preached a revival. During one of his services I was so moved by his message that I went forward and gave my heart and soul to Jesus Christ. From that time on, my life changed for the better. I found out that I had a pretty good voice and I began to sing in the choir. I also excelled in the RA's. I was moved from Greenwood Cottage to Eastover where I became acquainted with the chickens and a man named "Hawk" Hawkins.

Name two or three staff members that had a very special impact on shaping your life and character at Connie Maxwell.

I will be glad to name as my number one, Mr. Clyburn. He was a straight shooter.

Mr. Rhodes will always be in my memory as he was one of the strongest men I have ever known. He was always fair and I was never the recipient of any of his famous spankings.

Miss Grace Holtzclaw always had a smile for you. She demonstrated a dedication to duty like none I have ever seen.

Mr. Hawkins, who had the courage to admit that he was wrong when, by mistake, he whipped me for stealing money from his pockets. In fact, he gave me five cents for each lick he had whacked me.

Explain some things that happened to you that brought you success because of what you learned or experienced at Connie Maxwell.

When I entered the USAF, in 1952, I was sent to Lackland AFB, TX for basic training. Some of my fellow classmates had a terrible time with the daily routines, i.e., bed making, shoe shining, washing clothes, etc. I saw this as an everyday task and I managed to excel. In fact, I was so good that I was appointed squad leader. Connie Maxwell taught me all those chores.

My Christian walk has always led me to respect my fellow persons. Believe it or not some people still notice things like manners and correct salutations.

At Connie Maxwell, we were blessed with a wide variety of foods. I have never said, "I hate that stuff." I learned to like it all.

You cannot live with lots of kids and remain timid very long. As a result I have always found it easy to meet and talk with people of any race or creed. This has helped immensely in life's journey.

How was your cottage mother an influence on you?

I had a cottage mother named Miss Josie Hardin. She was a lovely person whom all the children loved. If you went to her with a problem she would always take time and comfort you. She was gifted with a sweet temperament and a soft voice. She was a Christian in the truest sense of the word. I would have loved to be her adopted son.

Did you play and sports at Connie Maxwell? What were they – How did they influence you while at Connie Maxwell and/or after you left Connie Maxwell?

I was never much of a "jock" while at Connie Maxwell. However, I did try some sports. One year Mr. Herring got Connie Maxwell into Little League Football. We had try-outs and I was picked as the quarterback. In one game I scored six touchdowns and I guess that is some kind of a record. We went on to a six-zero season.

As for sports on campus, I always tried out for all sports and was never more than third string in any of them. I was always too light.

As a marble player I was unsurpassed. At one time I owned three syrup cans full of marbles. No one could beat me at "nucks." I could really fire a marble.

Did you work on the farm and what are your thoughts about campus work --- good or bad?

As a young man at Connie Maxwell we were always required to work. As a little boy you did all types of housework and this was good because idle minds are a good place for the devil to do his work. When I got my first vacation my Mom could not believe how good I could do house work.

I later went to the chicken farm, and I can truly say that I learned to hate chickens and do until this day. That is not to say that I did not learn a whole bunch about "chickies." I learned to process them all the way to the meat packing facility.

What were some things you did in your free time on campus—go to town, go to the movies, work, play, etc.?

I was always attracted to the library during my free time. I loved to read about those far away places. No doubt this influenced my decision to join the Air Force. It is sad to know that the library is no longer there. I suppose if I had the money that this would be a first priority as my endowment. Children need GOOD books.

I also loved to build "skate scooters" (you first had to steal the skates.) To build one that would coast from the church down to the old school was quiet a feat. That turn at the bottom of the hill was really exciting! I often wound up in the ditch. We did not have much but we really had great fun.

If I failed to mention Anderson's Store it would be an omission of great forgetfulness. If you had a nickel or whatever it sure was nice to go there and see what you could get for your money. It was usually cigarettes. And then there was the "Old Man" just down the road from Anderson's that cooked candy every Sunday afternoon. You could smell it all the way over to Eastern Star. Yum, yum!!

How are the things you learned at Connie Maxwell still shaping your life today?

My walk with God started at Connie Maxwell and still continues until today. If you want to meet the people in your community that really count just go to church. Having always lived around lots of people, I never meet a stranger. I find that this serves me very well in my business today. Lastly, group living demands that you show respect for others with diverse opinions.

Did you go to college when you left Connie Maxwell? Did Connie Maxwell help you financially?

I did continue my education after leaving Connie Maxwell. I was fortunate to have access to many subjects in the Air Force, both in and out of my career field. I was able to compile many college credits through the Air Force Community College. After retiring from the Air Force I was able, under the GI Bill, to continue my studies at a local college in Tampa,

Florida. I completed a two-year program of studies in Business Administration. My annual income far exceeds anything that I would ever imagined. I never received any tutorial assistance from Connie Maxwell but I never asked.

What advice would you have for children that are at Connie Maxwell now?

Dear Fellow Brothers & Sisters: I am just an "old sinner" saved by His grace. I make no boast of my righteousness for I have none. If I should ever have any, it would belong to Jesus Christ.

I am writing you this note because I have a burden for "lost souls." In the event you do not know Jesus as your personal Savior, then sadly, you are a lost soul – a soul that is destined to spend all eternity in hell if you do not give your entire being over to His care.

I speak of hell because it is a place of reality, of such horror, that the human mind does not have words to adequately describe what takes place twenty-four hours a day for all eternity. Satan is the tormentor and he is a world class genius at what he does. Many things are known through the Word of God. For instance, all souls BURN in hell. The same senses that you were blessed with here on earth will be heightened in hell. The stench, the darkness, no food, no water, no sleep and the screaming of the damned goes on forever and ever.

I hope what has been said will prompt you to fall on your knees and repent of your sins and ask God, the Father, to forgive you. Tell Him that you want Jesus, as your friend and Savior. Please read your bible and pray often. There is a book in print that I would recommend for your reading information which is entitled "A Divine Revelation of HELL," by Mary K. Baxter, and it can be purchased @ amazon.com. I have not written this because I think I am better or more holy than any body. I have done so because I am my brother's keeper and I love you.

What adjustments have you made (if any) when you are asked, "Where were you raised?"

None. In fact I often brag about my roots with Connie Maxwell. At Christmas time this year I sent a gift to The Virginia Baptist Children's Home, and I mentioned my affiliation with Connie Maxwell. The Director of that home sent me a nice note saying he knew all about Connie Maxwell Children's Home. That really made me happy and proud!

--Joe Taylor

****

Personal Story - Gloria Ellis

In later years my mother, before she died, begged forgiveness for placing us at Connie Maxwell. I assured her many, many times that it was one of the best things she ever did and I was most grateful and had no regrets.

One thing I do know, if there had been no Connie Maxwell I would never have been a part of a happy, adjusted family life. I feel richly blessed and I thank God. Connie Maxwell was there for us and for many others who have passed through my life and are a part of the heritage of Connie Maxwell.

--Gloria Cook Ellis

****

Personal Story - Joe Redden

My dad had tuberculosis for over a year and I sold peanuts for almost two years until he died in January 1928. He was a Mason and suggested to mom that she contact the Masonic Home in Macon, Georgia. They replied that they were closing some cottages and weren't accepting any more children. Since he had a welding shop in Greenwood and was a member of the First Baptist Church, he suggested that she contact Dr. Jamison about admitting all five children. He stated there was a rule that no child over thirteen could be admitted. My sister, Katherine, was too old. So he suggested that she take the two girls, Katherine and Elizabeth to Atlanta to stay with her widowed sister, Aunt Lallah and place the three boys in Connie Maxwell, which was the best thing that has happened to me.

Ralph, Wallace, and I went to Connie Maxwell on March 10, 1928.

There were no negative experiences that happened to me that are worth mentioning. There were so many positives that they are too numerous to mention.

I'll try to be brief. I learned that Baptists do love children and do a super job in providing for them. I had new clothes, plenty of nourishing food, excellent health, proper dental care, good teachers, and a church that provided for my spiritual well being. We were given tasks that taught us to be punctual, to be polite, to be responsible for our own actions, and to take pride in doing a good job.

We learned to be responsible for those younger than we and to help them in every way possible. We learned how to get along with children of all ages, both in our own cottage and elsewhere on campus.

Mr. Jack Sheridan was one who stands out as an excellent role model. I enjoyed working in the print shop under his direction. Mr. Will Nixon, our dairy boss, was a wonderful Christian man whom I admired very much. I greatly admired Dr. A. T. Jamison, our superintendent and pastor, although I was never really close to him

<u>No one had a negative influence on me.</u>

I learned that I was responsible for my own well being. I broke my left leg on December 26, 1934, and spent a whole month in Greenwood Hospital.

That trip to the hospital placed me in jeopardy of having to repeat the tenth grade. I asked Major Benson, my principal, to ask my teachers to give me make-up work so I could pass that grade. He did and I did.

I played baseball, football, and basketball and ran track. I was the champ in chinning reaching fifty-six chins at one time.

I learned that you can pretty much achieve what you set as your goals; and that you do not have to rely on anyone else. This held me in good stead while I was in the aviation cadet program during World War II and stayed with me all the way through the twenty-nine years and ten months of my military career.

I can talk for hours in praise of my life at Connie Maxwell and I never get tired of letting people know how fortunate I am to have been provided for so well. My slogan is SHED NO TEARS FOR ME. Thanks for giving me this opportunity to speak well of my beloved home, Connie Maxwell Children's Home.

--Joe Redden

****

Personal Story - Rose Calder

What were some the circumstances that brought you to Connie Maxwell?

My family lived in rural Lee County when most people farmed and families were usually large. I had four brothers and one sister. Our mother died in March of 1934. Times were hard, but my father was never negative, always loving. He kept us together until 1939. By that time the two older boys were in C.C.C. camp or the Army. It took one year, August 1938 to September 1939 for Ethel, Lindy and myself to be accepted. Oh! That Sunday! When our neighbors the Watsons carried us to Greenwood. The first person we saw was Dr. Smith and then we were taken to number seventeen and Mrs. Vera Smith.

I'm sorry to say none of my aunts and uncles, who had smaller families, offered my father any help. I don't remember my grandmother being very loving or helpful after my mother's death. God blessed us with a good father. He never failed to visit us. He even saved sugar ration stamps for us during the war.

What were some positive experiences that you had at Connie Maxwell?

I was blessed with Miss Cooner as my teacher. You could differ with her. I remember that he also taught us good penmanship.

Dr. Smith brought out the best in us and encouraged us to do better. He gave me the chance to play basketball from the eighth grade till I graduated. He encouraged me to attend Lander but I felt I was needed at home to care for my father.

I was given the opportunity to attend Camp Rawls, the G.A. Camp, one summer and "Maw" Windham actually made me several new outfits to wear. Unheard of!

Dr. Murdock led me to accept Christ and baptized me. It was easy to talk with him.

Mr. Clyburn, I thought, understood us better than anyone else and had a "listening ear." He remained my friend until he died.

Explain some things that happened to you that brought you success because of what you learned or experienced at Connie Maxwell.

I learned to do my very best, to do it correctly, and to do it on time. These principles have carried me through my work, my church activities, my marriage of fifty-two years, and my dealings with people.

Did you play any sports at Connie Maxwell? What were they? How did they influence you while at Connie Maxwell and/or after you left Connie Maxwell?

I was a "Tom Boy" – played basketball and football with the boys. I did a lot of begging and Dr. Smith let me play softball on a mill team. I learned to be competitive, to be a good sport and to play fair.

What were some things you did in your free time on campus – go to town, go to the movies, work, play, etc.?

My father sent us money and we were able to get a ticket at the office for nine cents and attend the theater on Maxwell Avenue. We would go to the playground after supper. Richard Hightower was in charge of the canteen we had at the Ezell Gymnasium. We would hang with some boys who were in a special group – Lloyd Walker, Gene Cale, Beaver Hawkins and Bill McGill. I was the only girl allowed. We went to the woods near the dairy and made coffee in a can.

We were involved in Field Day where we had all sorts of races, dodge ball, etc. - very competitive with the other cottages.

We attended the baseball games on campus. We, also, enjoyed the annual Lions Easter Egg Hunt and going to the movie after the egg hunt.

How are things you learned at Connie Maxwell still shaping you life today?

Patience, my friend, patience! I never lost faith as a child and still hold fast that everything is for a purpose and God is still in control, allowing us to make decisions, some good and bad. South Carolina Baptists provided for my needs, not my wants, and I try to share my experiences when the opportunity presents itself.

I love to bake and without "much ado" I can prepare a full meal for families (twenty-five) when there is a death. My cooking for Eastern Star Boys and Girls prepared me well. I learned to hang loose and hang till the end – don't give up!

What advice would you have for children that are at Connie Maxwell now?

Take advantage of this precious time in your life. Realize we cannot always be where we would like to be, live with those we choose, or change the circumstances that brought us to this time in our lives. Be positive, it will carry you farther, make the ride smoother, and let time pass faster.

The world doesn't care for those who whine. Don't carry your feelings on your shoulders. Smile and speak to people. Yours may be the only smile others will receive.

Be Christ-like, even if it's not fashionable and popular.

What adjustments have you made (if any) when you are asked, "Where were you raised?"

I have always been proud of the opportunity afforded me to be a part of this great ministry to children. <u>I often wonder what might have happened had my father not loved us enough to part with us when he did.</u> I consider my church family a valued part of my life. My home church at one time sponsored nine children; and other local churches in our area clothed three others. I am a *Connie Maxwell* product and I'm proud of it!

I truly feel sorry that some children who grew up there do not acknowledge this now and don't want to be reminded of it – shame on them!

P. S. **After 108 years, Connie Maxwell is still doing it right**.

--Rose Rogers Calder

****

Personal Story – Leo Banks

My father died during the depression and my mother was unable to support us – thus we came to *Connie Maxwell*.

I'm sure there were some negative experiences but at the moment I can't recall them. One of the most positive experiences I had was a caring housemother. <u>She cared for</u>

me and she led me to accept Christ as my personal savior. At
the time I thought she was the meanest person in the world.

Three of my mentors who were always there for me were Dr.
Sam Smith, Miss Edith Wells, and Miss Susie Newbold.

Sports were a great teacher for me.   I played second base on
the baseball team and was the center for our football team,
which at the time was a six-man squad.   Our coaches were two
teachers from Greenwood High School.

I worked on the farm and at the dairy when I was at Connie
Maxwell. Most of my time was spent at the storeroom. I think
campus work should be mandatory for every child regardless
of the type of work it might be. I learned a lot at Connie
Maxwell but one of the most important things I learned was
that if you started a job, you should complete it.

I was an usher at the front door of the church. Every Sunday
when Mr. Nixon came up to the front door, he would always
say, "I would rather be a doorkeeper in the house of my God
than dwell in the tents of the wicked." (Psalm 84:10b-NIV) I
learned that good things come to those who put their trust in
the Lord. Each day I try to do His will.

I went to University of South Carolina for one semester after
I got out of the service. After one semester I was called back
into service in the Korean conflict.

The best advice I could give a child today is to study hard,
listen to your housemother and the staff.

I was and still am very proud to say that I was raised at Connie Maxwell Children's Home. The shaping of my life at Connie Maxwell has stayed with me all these years.

--Leo Banks

****

Personal Story - John Allen Sheriff

I was born in Pickens, South Carolina in 1945 and lived the first five years of my life in Liberty, South Carolina. As I reflect back to 1951, I see a family of 14 struggling to survive. My father, who was uneducated, tried to farm for a living. It was all he could do to feed us. My mother, also uneducated, had the ability to make you feel her love as no other person could ever make you feel. This dear lady, we called "Ma," was the strength that kept the family together. In 1951 she died from cancer. At the age of five, this was devastating, not only to me, but also to the whole family. My father, who loved his children, could see he needed help. He found that help at Connie Maxwell Children's Home. My father had the highest praise for Connie Maxwell, even until the day he died in 1980.

In November of 1951 six brothers came to Connie Maxwell with a pair of brogans (shoes), two pair of overalls, and a loving, caring father who paid to have someone bring his boys there. I will never forget the lonely, lost feeling I had that day when the car left the front yard at Cuthbert Cottage.

A dear lady by the name of Mrs. Goings was the cottage mother. She had more understanding than any one that I have

192

ever known. She was the best thing that ever happened to my five brothers and me. Mrs. Goings had a strong personality. She had the ability, knowledge, and wisdom to pass on her teaching through her counseling, actions, and her tough loving manner. I often heard her say, "You need to be an example to others," along with, "treat your fellowman as you want him to treat you." Another of her sayings was, "We need to keep ourselves in training, not only in body, but mentally and spiritually."

During the first several years at Connie Maxwell, I had a hard time adjusting to my new home. The house I came from had no running water, and the power stayed off most of the time because my father couldn't afford the payments. The big, wood frame house was heated with a fireplace in the winter. Water was drawn from a well in the back yard. Clothes were washed in a creek in front of the old, rundown house in the summer. In the winter months, clothing was washed in a big tub. It was always a struggle to have enough food to feed us.

I remember as a young boy at Connie Maxwell coming home from school and going to the screened-in front porch of our cottage to watch and see if my father was going to pick me up that day and take me back home. All the moving memories I had of home overcame me each day. I would cry until the cottage mother would come out and console me. I often wonder why I wanted to go home so desperately. I must have realized all the hardships at home, but that somehow didn't seem to matter. After several years I was able to accept my placement here at Connie Maxwell and grew to love it.

<u>I was baptized on Easter Sunday at the age of 8. This marked the beginning go my acceptance of being at Connie Maxwell. I</u>

have often thought of Connie Maxwell Children's Home as the personification of Peter and John. You will remember that Peter and John told the lame man at the temple gate to get up and walk after a life of being bed ridden. The staff has and will always continue to be willing to reach out to young boys and girls who are hurting physically, mentally, and spiritually. Connie Maxwell was here when I needed that help. I am trying to extend that same helping hand to other young people today.

During my stay at Connie Maxwell, I lived in four different cottages. All four of my cottage mothers were strong, compassionate, faithful women who instilled Christian values in me. For example, every Sunday morning each of us boys was required to recite a scripture verse before eating breakfast. I went to church on Sunday morning, Sunday evening, and on Wednesday nights. I was in Training Union every Sunday evening and participated in the church youth choir and the scout troop. In 1965, I was selected to be the Youth Week Pastor.

Sports were the contributing factor as to why I graduated from high school. I loved basketball, football, baseball, and track. I realized in order to play I had to keep my grades up. I graduated from high school in 1966.

Upon graduating from high school, I started working in the print shop at Park Seed Company. I was attending Piedmont Technical College in the evening. I wanted to be in the field of Technical Design or Drafting. The Vietnam War was going strong during that time and I received a draft notice from the Army to enter on November 22,1966. I was able to get into the National Guard on November 21, 1966, exactly one day before I was to report for boot camp. After my 6 months of active duty in the Army, I came home and applied for a job at the local newspaper, *The Index Journal.* Shortly after applying, I was hired to work in the composing room. Several weeks later, Mr. George Teasley saw me at church and said he wanted to talk to me. Mr. Teasley was the Home Life Director at Connie Maxwell. It seemed Mr. Teasley wanted me to be the coach for the mite and midget basketball, football, and baseball teams in the City and YMCA leagues. That day was one of the happiest days of my life. I had a job at *The Index Journal* and a part time job making $15 a month at Connie Maxwell. I worked at that part time job for 18 years (1967-1985.) I started out working with the younger students and after some years was given the responsibility of working and coaching our older teams.

In 1970, two big changes happened in my life. I was married to a former student, Sue Taft, and I was promoted at *The Index Journal.* I began working in the Circulation Department. In 1973, our first child, John David, was born. And that year brought another big change, my promotion at *The Index Journal* to City Circulation Manager.

In 1980, two other significant events occurred. I became an employee at the Print Shop at Connie Maxwell, where I had worked when I was a student. In July, our daughter, Christina Gail, was born. Since 1980, I have worked as the Work Pool Supervisor, and served as an Assistant to the Campus Administrator. I also served as a Team Leader and Director of Enrichment. In 1989, because of a restructuring at Connie Maxwell, I became the Jamison Team Leader. In 1995, I was appointed as the <u>first Director of Enrichment</u>.

I feel extremely fortunate to have the opportunity to give back something given to me many years ago as a young boy and as a young man growing up at Connie Maxwell. I appreciate the rewards of observing growth in both staff and students. I always look forward to teaching our students and the staff new ways of meeting their physical, emotional, social, and spiritual needs. This gives me personal and professional satisfaction. To see and hear successful stories of children gives me a great sense of pride.

Serving and sharing my faith in Christ Jesus with people has been one of my most meaningful contributions to children and their families. To motivate young people who have lost faith in themselves and each other is fulfilling. It gives me great pleasure to watch a young person improve his self-esteem. I also enjoy working with young people off campus. I have been involved in Junior Achievement, March of Dimes Walk-a-thon, Just Say No Walk-a-thon and served as Treasurer, Vice-President, and President of the Connie Maxwell Alumni Association.   At Connie Maxwell Baptist Church, I have served as a R.A. Leader, Sunday school teacher, Chairman of the Deacons, Children II Director, Church Custodian, and Chairman of the Church Ushers. I have served on the Personnel Committee, the Nominating Committee, and the Benevolence Committee. I have also been involved with Men's Fellowship and the Adult Choir.

Several years ago, we had a young man whose mother was in the hospital and his social worker called him into her office to explain his mother's condition to him. After he left her office, the social worker came to my office to inform me about the situation and to let me know the young man was upset. I left the office and picked him up on his way to work. Without saying a word, we went to the farm and parked the car. As I turned to him, he yelled, "Why is God doing this to me and my mother!" At that very moment his words hit a nerve with me. We both sat in the car holding each other as he cried. After a few minutes, we were able to talk openly about his feelings. I explained to him that God was not the cause of his mother's illness. I assured him that God loved him and would help him through this difficult time. He and his mother are both doing well today.

People often ask me what I feel my purpose is in life. I tell them it is to motivate people in the right direction and to help young people find direction and focus in their lives. Challenging young people to strive to be the best that they can be is also important. To give young people an opportunity to try new and challenging things is another purpose of my life. Sharing the good new of Jesus Christ, while being patient when I sometimes can't understand a young person, is something I try to do on a daily basis. One of the things that continues to motivate me is remembering the many different personalities who worked with me a young boy and remembering what was effective and what was not effective. I have tried to emulate the people that I have followed in the past. I list and remember how staff worked with the many different problems each day and how they solved them. I make sure each and every child is treated the same. I try to give each student the opportunity and motivation to be the best they can be. I see a lot of our children as underdogs and I want to help them overcome those afflictions that have put them in that position in the first place.

Each of us knows that conversion of the heart is the beginning of the most wonderful, eye opening experience that one will ever have. To help students find God is my primary motivation for everything I do at Connie Maxwell. My wish is for every student to come to know God in a personal and intimate way.

---John Sheriff

Author's commentary: John and Sue Sheriff are excellent testimonies of Connie Maxwell Children's Home. I have known John since 1951. I am extremely delighted that he is my brother and a fellow Connie Maxwell alumni. His and Sue's love of Connie Maxwell has enriched the lives of many, many young boys and girls and has helped them overcome the devastation of childhood experiences. A personal note to John and Sue: Your life, your commitment, your love, and your energy stands out like a shining beacon in a pitch dark night. You are very special people. I remember John quoting to me an old "saying" that goes something like this:

> "There's a destiny that makes us brothers; none goes his way alone. All that we send into the lives of others, comes back into our own."

****

"If my father and mother leave me, the Lord will take me in." Psalm 27:20 NIV

AND REMEMBER

**IF IT
IS TO BE,
IT IS
UP TO ME**

SO WHAT?

Chapter 11

Love has a way of tiptoeing up behind you only when you start sharing it with someone else. But there are people who think that approval should be rationed, so they keep it to themselves, and they don't like to do for others until others do for them.

If you measure out meanly your contribution against someone else's, you become a beggar and a trader instead of a giver, and responsibility becomes a duty, not a calling, and with it goes the magic and the delight.

I thought I would never get to this last chapter. Two years ago (June 1998) I had no idea what its title would be. I finally decided on the title, *"So What?"* I didn't make this decision until Saturday night, June 10, 2000. Dr. Jimmy McAdams made an excellent talk on *"Connie Maxwell and the Future."* In a heartbeat I realized that I would like to use some of those special things he talked about that night. All of us "old grads" of Connie Maxwell have talked from time to time about the same thing – would the Connie Maxwell we knew always be the special, positive influence it was for us? Will the present Connie Maxwell students have the same love and concern that we have? If it ever changed, how and why would it change? We found ourselves being a little jealous of our own experiences and feeling that the present students should be exposed to those same experiences. However, we also realized that things do change and we could not dictate to the present staff and students the things that "happened" to us.

I was talking to Dr. McAdams just recently about a trustee matter and mentioned to him that I would like to use the points he talked about in the speech he gave on June 10, 2000. He indicated to me that this last chapter could be entitled *"So What?"* I thought about what he had said for several days and realized that it was an ideal title for this final chapter.

I have thought long and hard about why I wanted to write a book about Connie Maxwell. I have come up with these answers:

1. I could not think of a book that I had ever read that described life and growing up in a home like Connie Maxwell.

2. I felt there was something deep in my soul that said, "The timing is right for you to take on this responsibility and let the world know what it was like to be raised in a Baptist Children's Home.

3. I felt I needed to speak for many other children, who, like me, were raised in a "children's home."

4. I felt like the timing was right to dispel the myth that children raised in an "orphanage" or "children's home" were some how permanently scarred for life and probably could not overcome that obstacle. That myth was very quickly dispelled. Almost all of the respondents who returned my questionnaire told of the many hardships they overcame and how it shaped their lives in a positive way. Several of them said they wouldn't change what happened to them even if they could. Some of the things that

they overcame warmed my heart, as I'm sure it did yours.

5. I felt if I talked to enough alumni who had lived at Connie Maxwell, I would be able to answer the question, "<u>Do they feel the same way I do</u>." I was amazed to find out that almost all of the respondents felt the same as I did – all of us were exposed to the inside story. We were on the inside looking out, not outside looking in. Society had almost always had the attitude <u>that "we need to feel sorry for those kids raised in an orphanage"</u> and I think it made some of us feel sorry for ourselves.

I have wandered many times where I might be today if I had stayed with my father in Greenville, SC. He worked in construction, was gone a good part of the time, was a heavy drinker, paid very little attention to any of his three children, and certainly was not a good role model. I'm certain I would have been considerably worse off under those conditions. Seeing some "homeless" adults and children "grub staking" on the streets is not a very pretty sight. Every time I see a homeless person I think of myself – but for the grace of God, Connie Maxwell, and the Baptists of South Carolina – there I go.

Here is the synopsis of the speech that Dr. McAdams gave to the alumni the evening of June 10, 2000.

"A year ago, Connie Maxwell trustees allowed Connie and I three months of traveling to all the children's homes operated by Baptists.

"We walked the streets of Williamsburg where our forefathers began dreaming about freedom and took great risk in order to claim it for themselves.

"We stood in the very church in Richmond where Patrick Henry inspired his fellow countrymen by declaring: "Give me liberty or give me death."

"We circled the belt way in the district of Columbia observing the Washington monument and the U. S. Capital, two great edifices that pull together thoughts of yesterday's leaders and today's leaders of the freedom pursuit.

"Twice we crossed bridges over the Mississippi, once we drove through a mountain tunnel, frequently we traveled roads made possible by the reshaping of mountains – all these symbols of America's determination to not be limited or separated.

"We passed through great stretches of painted desert to stand at last on the rim of the Grand Canyon. The feeling one gets observing that awesome spectacle is perhaps best expressed by the young boy who upon seeing the canyon for the first time was heard to say: "Man! Something must have happened here!"

"My appreciation for my country is certainly stronger this year than ever before. As Americans, you and I have a sacred trust to preserve, to mold, and to improve. Three goals: To see as much of her as possible; to often express thanks for the privilege of being an American; and to pray for those who pilot her future course.

"Now to the future of Connie Maxwell...

"An effective leader must maintain a proper balance of three time perspectives. He dare not fixate exclusively on the past, the present, or the future but must develop and practice a healthy appreciation for each dimension of an organization's life. For this presentation, however, I want to share my heart regarding the future of Connie Maxwell.

"To the degree that the trustees will approve it and Baptists and the staff will partner with me, the following strategic goals will direct our thinking, our planning, our praying, and our expenditure of energies and resources for making Connie Maxwell God's answer to children and families:

"We're going to strengthen our sense of community. We are a little microcosm of the world. We get a taste of every aspect of life: tensions, troubles, threats, problem solving, forgiving, failing, overcoming, conflict, disappointment, separation, and support.

"We're going to give priority to developing a strong staff. Can they think? Can they relate? Can they be a member of the team? Can they adopt a posture of service? Can they love? Can they be happy?

"We are going to "stay the course." We are not going to do a lot of new things. We are going to strengthen the old tried and true.

"We are going to nurture our supportive partners: churches, alumni, and individuals.

"We're going to offer so much good, that the bad will lose its power. We're going to silence the bad by amplifying the good. We cannot do much about the bad, but we can make sure some good things happen.

"We're going to build an environment of learning-make this a learning place. As staff, we are not learning a lot of new things, but how to do old things a lot better. What we want the children to learn: 1) How to value self and others. If they value self and others, peace and a peaceful existence will result. They will understand the need for giving and receiving forgiveness. They will know how to get along with others. 2) How to be quiet. 3) How to listen. 4) How to wait. Instant gratification rarely produces lasting pleasure. 5) How to work. 6) How to practice discernment - right and wrong, good and bad, friends and enemies, the valuable from the worthless. 7) How to make and keep promises. 8) How to walk with Christ. 9) How to pursue dreams. 10) How to leave a legacy."

---Dr. Jimmy McAdams

What an excellent blueprint for continuing the legacy of this "tender ministry."

This last chapter makes me think of a short story about a man who bought an old, run down farm. The soil had not been fertilized, the barns had not been painted, and, in general, the place was real mess. A minister who lived in the area came by one day after the barns and the house had been freshly painted. The beautiful white picket fence had been repaired and painted. The old farm really looked as if it were new. The minister stopped and told the farmer that he remembered when the farm was in really bad shape. Then he said, "The Lord really has blessed you, hasn't He." The old farmer thought for a minute and then said, "Yes, He has blessed me, and I'm grateful; but you should have seen this place when he had it all to Himself."

This story brings us to a very important word, *responsibility*. Not just our personal responsibility, but our responsibility to Connie Maxwell and its future.

If you don't believe you are responsible, be very careful about taking risks because you are likely to let yourself down at the very moment when you most need yourself and your best efforts.

You are responsible for everything in your life – all the successes and all the failures. Accept your successes with modesty and gratitude. Accept your failures as realities from which you must learn. If you accept responsibility, you have something to learn from everything and, therefore, you have the best chance of growing to meet the future.

When you take responsibility for your life, you assume responsibility for your past. Thus you can gain new insights. You don't need to make more mistakes. Look at yourself honestly and accept what you have done. You'll feel better about yourself and your future will be in your hands because you recognized your role in the past.

May we all take a closer look at ourselves and determine to move onward to a more fulfilling life in Christ Jesus.

The Man In The Glass

"When you get what you want in your struggle for self, and the world makes you king for a day, just go to the mirror and look at yourself and see what that man has to say.

For it isn't your father or mother or wife whose judgment upon you must pass. The fellow whose verdict counts most in your life is the one staring back from the glass.

You may be like Jack Horner and chisel a plum and think you're a wonderful guy. But the man in the glass says you're only a bum, if you can't look him straight in the eye.

He's the fellow to please – never mind all the rest, for he's with you clear to the end. And you've passed your most dangerous, difficult test, if the man in the glass is your friend.

You may fool the whole world down the pathway of years and get pats on the back as you pass. But the final reward will be heartache and tears, if you've cheated the man in the glass."

--Author Unknown

I sincerely hope this book has been as much of a blessing to you as it has been to me. I have proof read it several times and thought it would become "old hat" after the second or third reading; but, instead, I have gotten "cold chills" every time I have read it.

I have sensed in me a deeper level of responsibility to follow the points that Dr. McAdams outlined in his speech of June, 10, 2000: <u>to strengthen the sense of community; to give priority to staff; to stay the course; to nurture supportive partners; to offer so much good that the bad loses it power; and to build an environment of learning for Connie Maxwell.</u>

I am also reminded of what Rose Calder said when she closed her story: **"After 108 years, Connie Maxwell is still doing it right."**

I hope you will go back to the pages of this book more than once; and each time you do, that you will gain deeper insights about the people and events contained herein. That you will gain a deep and convicting love for "orphans" and for "orphanages" – May God continue to bless Connie Maxwell Children's Home.

AND REMEMBER,

IF IT
IS TO BE,
IT IS UP TO ME

"God is in his holy temple. He is a father to orphans, and He defends the widows." Psalm 68:5 NIV

"Wait on the Lord; be of good courage, and He shall strengthen your heart; wait, I say, on the Lord"

Psalm 27:14 NKJV

EPILOGUE

For over one hundred years the Baptists of South Carolina, through Connie Maxwell Children's Home, have opened their doors to thousands of children in need. Separation from family at any age is a frightful reality but more so at a young age. Children arriving at Connie Maxwell will begin a journey that will continue for a lifetime.

This book contains several stories of children that have undertaken this journey. A journey of compassion, caring, responsibility, fun, security, discipline, work ethics, sportsmanship, understanding, teamwork, spiritual and physical growth, and most of all love through services provided by the staff of Connie Maxwell Children's Home.

Journeys of success have taken students of Connie Maxwell to all parts of the world and into all walks of life. Their love and appreciation of Connie Maxwell is witnessed through attendance at the alumni reunion every two years and in unselfish giving to Connie Maxwell through its regular program, the Sam Smith Endowment, and the alumni association. Their journey has extended into the communities where they live with a commitment to pass on, through service, the love they were shown at Connie Maxwell.

Connie Maxwell Children's Home has met the challenge for all these years to the children that have made the journey through its care. It continues to meet the challenge today with its loving ministry to children in need throughout South Carolina. With God's help, Connie Maxwell will continue to provide a pathway for children of the future to make their journey into the next millennium of Christian living.

For God so loved the children of South Carolina – that he gave us Connie Maxwell Children's Home – that whosoever journeys through its doors – should never want – but have everlasting love.

-----Mack Baltzegar

"And above all things have fervent love for one another, for love will cover a multitude of sins.

I Peter 4:8 NKJV

ABOUT THE AUTHOR

James E. "Gene" Bishop is the President and founder of People &
Solutions, Inc. - a firm that provides the latest in training workshops
and seminars designed to enhance people to people communications
and the building of team skills.

He has an extensive background in the marketplace as an active
businessman. He is a well-known speaker, workshop director, and
team building counselor, working regularly with companies and other
groups to develop winning teams.

Gene is the past president of the Greer Chamber of Commerce;
Chairman of the Board of Trustees of Connie Maxwell Children's
Home, and a charter member of the Board of Directors of
Crimestoppers, Greenville, SC.

He is a member of Brushy Creek Baptist Church, Taylors, South
Carolina where he has served on the Board of Deacons, taught Sunday
school, and served on the Personnel Committee. He, along with his
wife, Pat, currently serves as the leader of the divorce recovery
program at Brushy Creek Baptist Church. Gene is also active in the
pre-school program and in the prayer ministry program at Brushy
Creek.

Gene is the author of two books, "*I Heard What You Didn't Say*" and
"*The Anatomy Of A Winning Lifestyle.*"

He is a native of Greenville, SC and received his education at North
Greenville College and Furman University. He is a member of the
Carolina Society of Training and Development and the International
Speakers Network. He is married to the former Pat Avants and has
four children and eight grandchildren.

His claim to fame is typing the discharge papers of the famous rock 'n
roll king, Elvis Presley.

"Let everything that has breath praise the Lord. Praise the Lord!
Psalm 150:6 NKJV

[1] Rethinking Orphanages for the 21st Century, pg. 2, Foreword

[2] Rethinking Orphanages for the 21st Century, pg. 6
  [7] As reported in A *Challenge for the Nation,* pg. 3

[3] Rethinking Orphanages for the 21st Century, pg. 6

[4] Rethinking Orphanages for the 21st Century, pg. 7

[5] Rethinking Orphanages for the 21st Century, pg. 7-8
  [14] John Seita, Martin Mitchell, and Christi Tobin,
In Whose Best Interest: One Child's Odyssey, A Nation's Responsibility
(Elizabethtown, Pa.: Continental, 1996), pp. 93, 96, 98, 100.

[6] Rethinking Orphanages for the 21st Century, pg. 8

[7] Rethinking Orphanages for the 21st Century, pg. 9
  [18] See Richard B. McKenzie, "Orphanage Alumni:
How They Have Done and How They Evaluate Their Experience." *Child and
Youth Care Forum,* April 1997, pp. 87-111. The overwhelming majority of the
respondents indicated that they maintain favorable assessments of their
orphanage experience.

[8] Rethinking Orphanages for the 21st Century, pg. 9

[9] Rethinking Orphanages for the 21st Century, pg. 13
  For a set of policy recommendations designed specifically to curb
child abuse, see Fagan and Hanks, "The Child Abuse Crisis."

Published by
People & Solutions, Inc.
108 Tanager Cr., Greer, SC 29650

For additional copies:
1-800-447-3698 or 864-244-5963
E-Mail: PSTrainU@aol.com

**All proceeds from this book
will be donated to the
Sam Smith Endowment,
Connie Maxwell Children's Home
Greenwood, South Carolina**